HUMAN RESOURCES SIMULATION
USING LOTUS® 1-2-3®

DR. LARRY E. PENLEY
Arizona State University

YOLANDA E. PENLEY
Chandler-Gilbert Community College

G832
PUBLISHED BY
SOUTH-WESTERN PUBLISHING CO.
CINCINNATI   WEST CHICAGO, IL   CARROLLTON, TX   LIVERMORE, CA

ISBN: 0-538-07832-4

1 2 3 4 5 6 **K** 3 2 1 0 9 8

Printed in the United States of America

PREFACE

Human Resources Simulation Using Lotus^{R}1-2-3^R is a text-workbook designed to aid students in enhancing decision-making skill and to teach them to use a human resources (HR) information system as a tool in making decisions. Students capable of understanding and using current technology, such as a HR information system, will make themselves more attractive candidates for employment to recruiters.

This text-workbook may be used as an adjunct to the college-level HR course and, as such, will provide students with the opportunity to make decisions that HR managers make in most organizations. This text-workbook may also be used as the primary book in a HR information system course.

Students and instructors will find that Human Resources Simulation Using Lotus 1-2-3 contains exciting exercises. This excitement comes from the text-workbook's ability to take students from the conceptual level of a HR textbook to the practical or applied level of making a HR decision.

Organizations are faced with increasingly greater demands for reporting information to state, local, and federal governmental agencies. A HR information system allows its users to design output screens so that the information may be provided directly from the system in a format that is acceptable to the government agency. This text-workbook employs two such exercises in which information is obtained from a database for meeting the demands of two government reports: the EEO-1 report and OSHA Form 200.

A HR department possesses important information that may be used to aid managers in making decisions with organization-wide implications. This text-workbook demonstrates the type of information (e.g., communication surveys) that may be provided from a HR information system for making organizationwide decisions, and it provides students with the opportunity to make such decisions.

Organizations face the need to respond quickly with complex information. In the midst of negotiations with a union, for example, representatives of management must be able to analyze the impact of proposals and counterproposals that union negotiators offer. A HR information system with its data on salaries and benefits for employees allows such "what if" questions to be answered. This text-workbook provides the opportunity to learn to use a HR information system in handling such immediate needs for complex information.

Users of this text-workbook will find an introduction to the HR information system in Chapter 1. That chapter includes information about the design of the text-workbook, as well as the Lotus 1-2-3 software upon which the simulation is based. Students and instructors who have never used a spreadsheet or who have never used Lotus 1-2-3 will gain a rudimentary understanding of Lotus 1-2-3, which will be required to perform the exercises contained in the remaining chapters of <u>Human Resources Simulation Using Lotus 1-2-3</u>.

Larry E. Penley
Yolanda E. Penley

CONTENTS

CHAPTER 1
MANAGING THE HUMAN RESOURCES INFORMATION SYSTEM

Chapter Outline

Computer-based human resources (HR) information systems are designed to make your life easier. They allow you to quickly obtain information that is difficult to find or unavailable without the database properties of computer-based systems. For example, they allow you to answer questions about an appraisal system which you could not answer without a HR information system that employs a database. The ability to answer such questions makes changing an appraisal system or an applicant-processing system easier. Moreover, access to information enhances the power that an HR information system has relative to the remainder of the organization.

For some time, large United States organizations have maintained computer-based files about their employees. These large organizations have been able to maintain these files for two reasons. First, they already possessed large mainframe computers; second, they have had large staffs of programmers and analysts to aid their HR managers. Smaller businesses have been left with more traditional written records of their employees.

Technological Changes in Information Management

Three interrelated technological changes have had an impact on the management of HR information in small and large organizations. First, the advent of the microcomputer has made available reasonably priced hardware--the computer itself--for managing information. Second, software--the instructions for the computer--has been designed which allows HR managers to store, manipulate, and retrieve information relatively easily. The ease of information storage, manipulation, and retrieval comes from the system's database properties that form its core. Finally, rapid improvements in hardware have made the speed of microcomputer operations sufficiently high and the capacity for storage sufficiently large for easily managing large amounts of information.

---

*Lotus^{R}1-2-3^R is a trademark of Lotus Development Corporation. Any reference to Lotus 1-2-3 refers to this footnote.

The Importance of Databases

A **database** is a computer file of a large amount of information. It is stored in a way that allows a user flexibility in rapidly obtaining information about a specific group of records within the file. A **record** is the information about an individual employee in a HR database. Typically, a record is stored as a <u>row</u> of information. Each record is organized so that certain categories of information about each employee are stored in association with a given field name. Usually, a **field** is a <u>column</u> of information on the same topic--e.g., salaries of employees. With a database, you can list all of the records (employees) that are similar with regard to some field. For example, you can list all of the employees (records) who are in grade three of the compensation system; <u>Grade</u> is an example of a field.

Small businesses may now use HR databases to follow the application process, record results of appraisals, make changes in a compensation system, evaluate a union wage and benefit proposal, etc. Just a few years ago these were activities that only the larger organizations could perform easily and rapidly. Even then, large organizations often were unable to conduct these activities despite the available hardware and software. Typically, computer time as well as programmer time were shared with other organizational functions such as finance and accounting. This shared resource was often available to HR personnel only when it was not required for those "essential" financial and accounting uses. Moreover, even when these resources were available to large organizations, there were severe limitations on the flexibility of the software.

With current database software, you can now add a new field to an employee record very easily. For example, you can decide that you should start storing the results of annual appraisals. Since you already have a database on a microcomputer, you merely create a new field--e.g., Appraisal Score. You can then store some value for each employee in association with the field name <u>Appraisal Score</u>. With older mainframe computers, accomplishing this simple task meant that programmers had to be called in to modify the program. In many cases, this seemingly simple change could result in a series of changes, and the cost would rise enormously. Such costs, as well as the availability of the programmers to make the changes, meant that HR databases which did exist were inflexible and difficult to manage. For the most part, they served as very limited <u>report generators</u> rather than as managerial tools.

Today many organizations are using specially designed HR databases to manage the growing information that must be retained about each employee. In addition to making the management task easier, databases are able to ask questions which formerly were very difficult to ask. At one time, the task of determining the number of employees who fell into the various EEO (Equal Employment Office) categories was not a small task. Now, many HR databases can do this in seconds and print the results in a form that is acceptable as a substitute for the official government report form.

Such HR databases are increasingly visible among HR professionals. At the annual meetings of the ASPA (American Society for Personnel Administration), special sessions about managing computer-based HR information systems are conducted. There are booths with vendors who sell HR software that allows a person to manage databases. Personnel and Personnel Administrator--the periodicals that many HR professionals read--contain advertisements and articles associated with HR information systems.

These changes in the HR area are affecting the education of students who wish to enter the HR profession. Students must be familiar with the concepts of HR databases, and they must know the fundamentals of how to use a HR database. However, becoming familiar with the concepts and fundamentals of HR databases does not mean that a student will be able to immediately use the particular HR information system that any given organization possesses. The variety of HR information systems grows each year, and each system has unique characteristics. Still, all of them use a database as their core, and they work on the basis of similar principles. Fortunately for students, these principles can be easily learned with practice.

Focus of This Book

This book is designed to aid students in using a HR information system by becoming familiar with the concepts and fundamentals of a HR database. It presents various common inquiries and problems that a HR manager confronts, and it offers students the opportunity to obtain the information necessary for making decisions and resolving problems.

To simulate the situations faced by HR managers in a typical organization, a single organization was chosen as the basis for all of the exercises. That organization is Metro Hospital, a private hospital which is a subsidiary of a larger corporation. Information about a selected group of employees forms the foundation of the database. A large number of fields have been chosen in which to record information about the employees. For example, there is a field called Salary. For each employee, specific salary information is stored in association with that field.

Individual exercises draw on a slice of the large HR database. Using a portion of the database makes analyses easier in this learning environment, and it simulates the situation a HR manager faces. For example, a HR manager who is interested in the applicant-flow process for the job of staff nurse would probably begin by looking only at the slice of the database in which information about staff nurses is stored. Selecting data from only this slice of the database increases the speed of responses to queries, and it avoids the subsequent deletion of information about other job categories as queries are made of the database.

Using Lotus 1-2-3 with This Book

Lotus 1-2-3 is the software that you will use for your analyses of HR exercises in this book. One of the most common uses of Lotus 1-2-3 is as an electronic spreadsheet--a computer-based substitute for a large sheet of accounting paper. Lotus 1-2-3 contains rows and columns just like a piece of accounting paper that is used in completing accounting and financial analyses.

Lotus 1-2-3 also has the capability to perform database manipulations of stored information. This capability is one of the prime reasons for its use in association with this book. In addition, Lotus 1-2-3 allows you to easily perform calculations on the data that are stored in the spreadsheet.

Although you do not have to know very much about Lotus 1-2-3 to use this book, some familiarity with the way an electronic spreadsheet functions is required. Chapter 2 of this book is an introduction to Lotus 1-2-3. As you are assigned chapters from this book, you will find that early chapters provide greater detail about how to use Lotus 1-2-3 in order to solve a problem or obtain some information than do later chapters. Thus, a student having some familiarity with Lotus 1-2-3 will probably be able to begin work on the first exercise contained in Chapter 3. If you have never used an electronic spreadsheet or Lotus 1-2-3, you should find Chapter 2 a helpful beginning for accomplishing the exercises in this book.

Exercises in the Student's HR Data Diskette

A chapter of this book will be associated with each one of the exercises on the data diskette. Each data diskette contains an area of the spreadsheet called the **output screen**. This is the area in which you will complete certain calculations or "write" the results of your database manipulations. Thus, the output screen is the portion of the spreadsheet that you must print for your instructor's review.

Databases sort, select, and organize information, but they do not make decisions for the user. Therefore, questions that focus your attention on the issues that led to your analyses are presented in a page at the end of each chapter. As a part of each assignment, your instructor will ask that you answer these questions in the space provided, tear out the page, and hand it in along with the printed results of your analyses.

Required Resources

Here are the resources that you will need to complete the exercises contained in this book:
1. IBM PC, XT, or AT or a compatible computer.
2. 256K bytes of RAM memory.
3. Two floppy disk drives or one floppy and a hard disk.
4. A printer.
5. Lotus 1-2-3 diskette.
6. HR Student's Data Diskette.

Conclusion

A HR database is an essential tool for the management of HR information today. Your efforts to deal with the HR exercises in this book will aid you in preparing for the demands of a HR department in a modern organization. While gaining expertise in dealing with a HR database, you will also gain expertise in using one of the most widely available spreadsheets, Lotus 1-2-3.

CHAPTER 2
AN INTRODUCTION TO LOTUS 1-2-3

Chapter Outline

The purpose of this chapter is to provide you with basic information about the use of Lotus 1-2-3. This chapter is not designed to provide an in-depth understanding of Lotus 1-2-3, nor is it designed to cover all of the Lotus 1-2-3 functions that you will use with this book. Early chapters of this book (beginning with Chapter 3) assume that you have read this chapter; later chapters assume that you have gained some skill with Lotus 1-2-3. Therefore, the basic information presented in this chapter is not repeated in the later chapters. However, where a "new" statistical function or Lotus 1-2-3 command is introduced in a later chapter, a detailed explanation of its use is included in that chapter.

Getting Started

In order to gain the most from this chapter, you should read it while working at a computer. By doing so, you will be able to practice as you read. If you are using a dual floppy IBM PC or compatible computer, place the Lotus 1-2-3 system diskette in drive A, place your copy of the HR Data Diskette in drive B, and turn on the computer. If you are working with a hard disk or a network, you will need to ask your instructor or the computer laboratory assistant for help in accessing Lotus 1-2-3. Respond to any prompts which request that you enter the date and time. In a few seconds, you will see the opening Lotus 1-2-3 menu, accompanied by the words **LOTUS Access System.** Below these words will be the following choices for this menu:

1-2-3 File-Manager Disk-Manager PrintGraph Translate Exit

This menu responds to your choice of its options just as any later Lotus 1-2-3 menu does. Use the cursor (arrow) keys in order to move from left to right, and vice versa, in selecting a menu option.

If Lotus 1-2-3 beeps while you are trying to move the cursor, you may have the Number Lock on. If the Number Lock is on, the following message will be highlighted at the bottom of the screen:

Press [Num Lock]

The Number Lock key works like a toggle switch, alternately allowing you to use the same set of keys (on many computers) as numbers or cursor keys.

Notice that moving the cursor highlights one of the choices on the main menu. You may select a choice by pressing the Enter key (which is also the Return key) when that choice is highlighted. You may also select one of the choices by typing the first alphanumeric character (letter or number) of the choice. For example, you may enter the Lotus 1-2-3 spreadsheet by highlighting 1-2-3 and pressing the Enter key, or you may type the number 1. Either method will produce the same results.

The Worksheet

After moving past the opening menu and the copyright screen (for earlier versions of Lotus 1-2-3), you will see a screen that is mostly blank except for a series of letters (beginning with A across the top of the screen) and a series of numbers (beginning with 1 along the left side of the screen). You are looking at a portion of the worksheet which is visible at this moment. You are in the Ready mode, and in this mode you can begin to enter data, labels, and formulas into the worksheet.

Moving About the Worksheet. The four cursor (arrow) keys allow you to move about the worksheet as well as from one menu choice to another. Use them now to move from one cell of the screen to another.

As you try to use the cursor keys to move around the worksheet, you may encounter a problem. Pressing a cursor key may cause a number to be written in the upper left of the screen. This means that the Number Lock is toggled on. You must press the [Num Lock] key to toggle it off. As you do so, you will notice that the highlighted word **NUM** in the lower right of the screen will disappear. You should now be able to move about the worksheet by using the cursor keys.

You may move the cursor beyond the limits of the worksheet which are visible on the monitor. For example, move the cursor to the right until you are in column I. As you move the cursor to the right or downward, you will see additional areas of the worksheet. You may move the cursor to the next cell that contains data or to the end of a row or column by pressing the End key (shared with the number 1 on some computer keyboards), followed by one of the arrow cursor keys. Try this now by pressing the End key and the left cursor key. Notice that Lotus 1-2-3 moves the cursor to column A in the same row at which the cursor was located when you pressed the End key and the cursor key.

In addition to the cursor keys, you may move to another part of the worksheet with the Page Up (Pg Up) key and the Page Down (Pg Dn) key. Pressing the Pg Dn key moves the cursor down 20 lines, and pressing the Pg Up key moves the cursor up 20 lines. Try the Pg Dn and the Pg Up keys now.

Knowing Cell Addresses. A **cell** is defined by its address. In the upper left of the monitor screen, you will see the address of the cell in which the cursor is located. The very top left cell is called A1 since it is in column A and row 1. To become familiar with cursor movement and cell addresses, it is helpful to move the cursor about the screen in front of you while observing the change in cell addresses which is noted at the upper left of the screen. Try moving to several different cells while observing the cell addresses. When you press the Home key (shared with the number 7 on the number pad on some computer keyboards), the cursor will always return to cell A1.

Writing on the Worksheet. Move the cursor to cell A1 and type a number such as 352. Notice that nothing happens to the cell; however, the number 352 is visible near the upper left of the screen, just below the cell address. This area of the worksheet below the cell address is called the **edit entry line.**

If you make an error in typing something in the edit entry line, you may erase the error with the backspace key. Assume that the number 352 on the edit entry line is in error. You really wanted the number 35. Therefore, strike the backspace key once, and the 2 will disappear.

Do not use the cursor arrow keys for erasing an error; they will move the cursor to a new cell on the worksheet. Whatever you had entered on the edit entry line will be displayed at the current cell address. In fact, moving the cursor to another cell is one of two ways to transfer an entry from the edit entry line to the cell on the worksheet itself. The other way is to press the Enter key. If you have not pressed the Enter key, do so. If you had made an error and tried to use the cursor key to erase the 2 from the edit entry line, you may correct the error after reading the next section of this chapter.

Editing the Contents of the Worksheet. There are ten function keys on your keyboard. The second function key, F2, is the edit key. Let us suppose that you made an error in typing a label. The label should read DEPARTMENT, but you misspelled the word and had entered DEPARMTENT from the edit entry line into cell D4. Move the cursor to cell D4 and type this word with its incorrect spelling; now press the Enter key. Since it is too late to erase the error by using the backspace key while the error is still visible on the edit entry line, you must edit this error.

With the cursor at cell D4 (containing the misspelled word DEPARM-TENT) highlighted, press the F2 key. You can now move the blinking cursor on the edit entry line under the letters you wish to change. Simply use the left cursor key to move the cursor under the letter M and press the Delete key to eliminate this M. Now move the cursor key under the second E and type M to insert this letter in its proper location. Then press the Enter key, and the changed word or value will be reentered into its cell.

Rather than edit an entry, you may also replace an entry. For example, you could have moved the cursor to cell D4 and have retyped the word DEPARTMENT with the correct spelling. This action would have resulted in the misspelled word's having been replaced with the correctly spelled word.

Cell Entries

Lotus 1-2-3 recognizes two types of cell entries: **values** (numbers and formulas) and **labels**. This distinction is an important one for Lotus 1-2-3 since only values are subject to mathematical operations.

Values. The first character that you enter in a cell identifies it as a value or a label. Entering any of the following characters will identify the entry as a value:

1   2   3   4   5   6   7   8   9   0   .   +   -   @   # $ (

Numbers are values; they must begin with the number itself, a decimal point, or a dollar sign ($). Formulas are also values. They must begin with one of the following symbols that Lotus 1-2-3 identifies with a formula:

+   -   @   # $ (

Labels. Entering any other character will result in Lotus 1-2-3's treating an entry as a label. Enter any label, such as your last name, in a cell. Notice how the label looks in the upper left of the screen. It is no longer on the edit entry line. Since it now appears in a cell on the worksheet, it will appear after the cell address in the upper left of the screen as long as the cursor is at that cell. If you wish to change the spelling of your name at this point, you must edit the entry by pressing the F2 key while the cursor is at the cell in which your name is located.

Notice beside the cell address in the upper left of the screen that there is an apostrophe (') before the first letter of your name. This is a code that Lotus 1-2-3 uses to identify a cell entry as a label. Two other codes identify cell entries as labels: ^ and ". The ^ may be entered as the first character in a label, and the label will be centered within the cell. The " as the first character in a label results in the entry being justified to the right of the width of a cell. The default code is the ' which causes the entry to be justified to the left. If you type a label without any code as the first character, Lotus 1-2-3 will automatically enter the '.

Mixing Values and Labels. If you try to mix values and labels, you can create some difficulty for yourself. For example, if you try to enter your street address by beginning with the house or apartment number followed by the name of the street, Lotus 1-2-3 will beep at you. Lotus 1-2-3 does not know how to treat this entry since it appears to be a value because it begins with a numeral; yet, it also contains alphabetic characters like a label.

After beeping, Lotus 1-2-3 will automatically activate the Edit mode. In the Edit mode, the left and right cursor keys will no longer move about the worksheet, but will allow you to move within the edit entry line. The Enter key will not work either. You must correct the entry in the Edit mode by typing a ', ^, or " as the first character of the edit entry line. Lotus 1-2-3 will then accept the entry entirely as a label. Of course, you may also press the Escape key, and Lotus 1-2-3 will ignore the attempt to enter the address and retain the original cell entry or the blank cell, whichever preceded the attempt to type the address.

Mathematical Operations

The basic mathematical operations are indicated by the following common signs that indicate addition, subtraction, multiplication, and division, respectively:

$$+ \quad - \quad * \quad /$$

You can complete a modest example of the use of these mathematical operators by choosing one of the blank cells on your worksheet screen and entering a simple mathematical problem. For example, enter the following in one of the cells:

38+54

Notice that the cell on the worksheet will contain the sum of these two numbers: 92. Notice also that the original numbers (38+54) appear in the upper left of the screen even though the sum 92 is written into the worksheet.

The Order of Calculations. Lotus 1-2-3 orders its calculations by completing multiplication and division before it completes addition and subtraction. Thus, the following problem:

$$16-4/2+2$$

results in the -4 being divided by 2; then the result (-2) is added to 2 and subtracted from 16. The number you will see on your screen if you enter this mathematical problem is 16.

The Use of Parentheses. Sometimes parentheses are useful in performing several mathematical operations within the same cell. The purpose of the parentheses is to assure that calculations are completed as you intended them. For example, enter the following mathematical operation with the appropriate parentheses:

$$(16-4)/(2+2)$$

The result will be very dissimilar; it will be 3. The reason for the dissimilarity is that the parentheses control the order of calculations. Thus, 4 is subtracted from 16 before the difference (12) is divided by the sum of 2+2.

Parentheses are commonly used in Lotus 1-2-3, and you will find that they will be necessary for many of your entries. However, you must be careful to assure that every left parenthesis is balanced by a right parenthesis, and vice versa. If the parentheses are not balanced, Lotus 1-2-3 will beep at your attempt to press the Enter key, shift to the Edit mode, and refuse to accept the entry until the parentheses are balanced.

Use of Formulas

To learn to use formulas, you will need to enter some data into the worksheet. Type the following labels and numbers in the designated cells in order to simulate a database. Do not worry if you already have information in these cells; you will be able to replace that information with the desired entries displayed below.

	A	B	C
10	SALARY	BENEFITS	PERCENTAGE
1	36983	4093	
2	54159	4093	
3	17815	4093	

To calculate the percentage of salary that benefits represent, enter the following mathematical operation in cell C11:

$$4093/36983$$

Similar calculations can be performed for each subsequent line by changing the divisor (36983) and entering the mathematical operations in cells C12 and C13. You are now using Lotus 1-2-3 essentially as a cal-

12

culator.

Fortunately, Lotus 1-2-3 makes these repeated entries with separate divisors unnecessary. A formula can be created to perform the calculations. Instead of entering 4093/36983 in cell C11, the following formula serves very well:

+B11/A11

Similarly, in cell C12 the formula will be +B12/A12; in cell C13 the formula will be +B13/A13. Notice that each formula begins with the plus sign (+). This is a symbol which lets Lotus 1-2-3 know that you do not intend the cell entry to be a label; it is to be a value, i.e., a formula.

Formulas may employ any of the mathematical operators (+, -, *, and /) about which you have already read. Thus, the following formula is an acceptable one:

((B6/A6)*100)+(D6−E6)

This formula demonstrates several qualities of Lotus 1-2-3 formulas. They may begin with a left parenthesis rather than a +. Parentheses must be balanced on the left and right; thus, there are three left parentheses and three right parentheses.

Finally, this example demonstrates that formulas may be complex with several mathematical arguments. If you try the formula, you will get an error without values in cells A6, B6, D6, and E6. Lotus 1-2-3 will enter ERR in the cell in which you type this formula since you are dividing by zero.

Lotus 1-2-3 Command Menus

Lotus 1-2-3 has a series of commands which allow you to move cell entries about on the worksheet, copy formulas from one section of the worksheet to another, extract data from a database, etc. These commands are contained in a series of menus. You can access these menus by typing / (the slash or the symbol for division). Any Lotus 1-2-3 command begins with a /. When you type a /, you will observe the main Lotus 1-2-3 menu just under the cell address at the top of the screen. These commands will quickly become familiar to you because of their natural names. Each of the commands represents an additional submenu of commands. Here is a list of the main menu commands with the meaning of each:

13

Command	Meaning
WORKSHEET	includes commands that affect the entire worksheet, such as erasing the entire contents of a worksheet
RANGE	includes commands which affect only a part of the worksheet, such as erasing the contents of a group of cell entries or a limited area of the worksheet
COPY	permits copying any part of the worksheet to another area of the worksheet
MOVE	permits moving the contents of any part of the worksheet to another area of the worksheet
FILE	permits retrieving a stored worksheet or saving a stored worksheet before quitting Lotus 1-2-3
PRINT	permits printing any part of the worksheet
GRAPH	permits graphing data contained in the worksheet with a variety of charts and graphs
DATA	permits the sorting of data and the use of data as a database for data retrieval
QUIT	allows the user to quit Lotus 1-2-3 and return to the computer's operating system but does not save the contents of the worksheet

After typing / to see the main menu commands, notice that you can move the left and right cursor keys to each of the commands on the first line. As you do so, the commands on the second line change. The commands on the second line are associated with whichever main menu command is highlighted. You may select a command by moving the cursor and pressing the Enter key or by typing the first alphanumeric character of the command (e.g., R for RANGE). The commands which will be used with this book are discussed in subsequent sections of this chapter.

The Powerful Erase Command. A very powerful and dangerous Lotus 1-2-3 command is /WE (WORKSHEET ERASE). This command allows you to erase everything in the active worksheet. Try using this command now. If you still have the Lotus 1-2-3 main menu command at the top of the screen, type WE (WORKSHEET ERASE). If the main menu command is not at the top of the screen, type /WE (WORKSHEET ERASE). Due to the power of this command, Lotus 1-2-3 wants to make sure that you wish to erase the active worksheet. Thus, Lotus 1-2-3 will respond with another menu containing the following two commands:

No   Yes

Since you want to erase the entire worksheet, type Y (YES). Once you have responded with Y (YES), Lotus 1-2-3 will return to the Ready mode.

The Time—Saving Copy Command. Despite the ability to use formulas (e.g., +B2/A2) rather than actual numbers (e.g., 4093/36983) in a previous example, you probably noticed that there was little time saved by using the formulas over the numbers themselves. If you are entering only a few formulas, the difference in time is almost negligible. Of course, fewer errors occur in typing formulas than in typing numbers of several digits.

Fortunately, Lotus 1-2-3 offers you the ability to avoid wasting time in typing the additional formulas and to assure accuracy in entering them. It does this with the Copy command from the Lotus 1-2-3 main menu commands.

Return to the problem of calculating the percentage of salary represented by benefits. Since you erased the worksheet, you will have to enter the following information in columns A, B, and C and rows 10 through 13 of the worksheet:

	A	B	C
10	SALARY	BENEFITS	PERCENTAGE
11	36983	4093	
12	54159	4093	
13	17815	4093	

As you did earlier, enter the first formula. In this case, the formula +B11/A11 should be entered in cell C11. Observe that the cell contains the same result that you saw before:

0.110672

You can now copy this formula to cells C12 and C13, and Lotus 1-2-3 will automatically change the addresses of the copied formulas so that they correspond with the appropriate row. Move the cursor to cell C11 where you have typed the formula; type / to access the Lotus 1-2-3 main menu. Select the Copy command. (A quicker way to access the Copy command is to type the first alphanumeric character of the word--in this case, C.) Lotus 1-2-3 will prompt you with the following:

Enter range to copy FROM: C11..C11

Lotus 1-2-3 initially assumes that you want to copy from the cell at which the cursor is located, C11 in this case. Since you want to copy from only one cell, C11, press the Enter key.

If you had not previously located the cursor on cell C11, you would have had two choices. You could have (1) typed C11.C11, or (2) pressed the Escape (ESC) key, moved the cursor to cell C11, and pressed the Enter key.

Notice that Lotus 1-2-3 now prompts you with the following:

Enter range to copy TO: C11

Move the cursor to cell C12, type a period, and move the cursor down to cell C13. Observe that cells C12 and C13 are highlighted and that the prompt now reads:

Enter range to copy TO: C12..C13

Press the Enter key, and Lotus 1-2-3 will modify the formula as it copies the formula to cells C12 and C13.

An alternative response to the following prompt is to have typed C12..C13 and pressed the Enter key:

Enter range to copy TO: C11

When you know the range that you want to copy to, typing the address of the cells to which you wish the formula copied is the easier way.

Special Keys

The Escape (ESC) Key. If you make a mistake and press the wrong key in choosing from among the options or subcommands of one of the menus, use the Escape (ESC) key. Occasionally you may find that you need to press the Escape key several times in order to extract yourself from a series of submenu options. Continue pressing the Escape key until you return to the Ready mode without any of the Lotus 1-2-3 menus at the top of the screen.

The Help (F1) Key. If you need some help while using Lotus 1-2-3, press the F1 key. Lotus 1-2-3 will then present a screen of helpful information. Since Lotus 1-2-3 keeps track of what you are doing, the particular help screen which is presented will vary, depending upon the task.

Most of the help screens contain key words for which you can obtain additional information. Use the cursor keys to highlight the key word about which you want additional information. Then press the Enter key to obtain additional information.

You can leave a help screen by pressing the Escape key. Lotus 1-2-3 will return you exactly to the point at which you were working before you pressed the F1 key to obtain help.

Lotus 1-2-3 Statistical Functions

Statistical functions may sometimes substitute for formulas, and some statistical functions allow you to perform tasks that cannot be accomplished with formulas. Statistical functions perform such duties as calculating an average or mean of a list of numbers. They always operate on cell addresses that outline an area of the worksheet.

Each Lotus 1-2-3 statistical function begins with the symbol @. Each function then names the particular type of operation (e.g., SUM for sum or total) and contains an **argument**(s) within parentheses. The purpose of an argument is to identify the area of the worksheet on which the designated operation is to occur.

In the example with which you have been working, you could have used a statistical function in cell A14 to have added the three salaries. The entry in cell A14 would have looked like this:

@SUM(A11..A13)

This Lotus 1-2-3 statistical function is called **@SUM**; it adds the numbers found in the argument, i.e., the area of the worksheet identified within the parentheses.

The entire list of Lotus 1-2-3 statistical functions includes the following:

Statistical Function	Meaning
@AVG (area)	finds the average or mean
@COUNT (area)	counts the items in the area
@MAX (area)	finds the largest item in the area
@MIN (area)	finds the smallest (or most negative) item in the area
@STD (area)	finds the standard deviation
@SUM (area)	sums or adds the values in the area
@VAR (area)	finds the variance

Retrieving and Saving Files

Up to now, you have worked only in the Ready mode without importing a stored file as the active file. In this section of Chapter 2, you will learn how to retrieve and save files from the HR Data Diskette.

If your copy of the HR Data Diskette is not in drive B of your computer, place it in the drive and close the drive. You can now use the Lotus 1-2-3 commands to retrieve a file from the diskette and save any changes to the file. Before retrieving any files from your HR Data Diskette, make sure that you have a formatted, blank double-sided, double density diskette available. If you do not have one available, you should not proceed with this chapter.

Retrieving the Sample File TUTOR. Type /FR. The / accesses the main menu; the F (FILE) accesses a set of commands from the FILE submenu; and the R (RETRIEVE) allows you to retrieve a particular file from the data diskette. A series of files from the HR Data Diskette will be listed near the top of the screen below the following prompt:

Name of file to retrieve:

At this prompt you will need to continue moving the cursor to the right until the file TUTOR is highlighted. Press the Enter key to retrieve this file. Lotus 1-2-3 will flash the word WAIT in the upper right corner of the screen as it retrieves this file. When Lotus 1-2-3 returns to the Ready mode, the word READY will appear where WAIT was flashing, and the upper left part of the file which fits on the screen will be visible. At this time you should remove your HR Data Diskette and insert the formatted, blank "Working Diskette" which you have available.

The file you have retrieved (see Exhibit 2-1) is a sample file that contains data about several employees in the HR Database. This file contains some of the elements that you will find in all files with which you will work in this book. Cell A1 contains the Lotus 1-2-3 name of the file, TUTOR. Cell A2 contains the name of the chapter on which you are working, and cell A3 contains the highlighted word **Name:**.

As with each exercise you complete in this book, move the cursor to cell A3. Press the F2 key to edit the contents of this cell. Type your name and press the Enter key. You will see that your name is entered in the edit mode after the word **Name:** in cell A3.

Saving a File. You can now save this modified file onto the blank, formatted diskette that you inserted into the drive. This is called your "Working Diskette." Type /F (FILE) to access the FILE commands of the main Lotus 1-2-3 menu. Type S (SAVE) to save this modified file.

You must always save a file prior to quitting Lotus 1-2-3; otherwise any changes you have made to the active file will be lost. After having typed S (SAVE), Lotus 1-2-3 will prompt you with the following message, with some minor variations from system to system and from one version of Lotus 1-2-3 to another:

Enter save file name: TUTOR

Press the Enter key in order to tell Lotus 1-2-3 that this is the filename under which you want to save this worksheet. Lotus 1-2-3 will then save the file onto your Working Diskette. If you were to retrieve the file TUTOR from your Working Diskette and then tried to save it a second time onto the Working Diskette, Lotus 1-2-3 would return the following two sub-commands:

CANCEL   REPLACE

Exhibit 2-1

TUTOR
An Introduction to Lotus 1-2-3
Name:

DATABASE

NAME	DATE OF HIRE	DATE OF BIRTH	RACE	SEX	JOB TITLE	DEPARTMENT	EXEMPT	FACTOR	GRADE	STEP	ANNUAL SALARY
Abbott, Paula	17-Sep-76	20-Jun-37	W	F	LPN	OBGYN	N	401	6	7	19895
Abel, Judy	18-Apr-75	21-Jul-37	B	F	Histotechnician	MEDICAL LABORATORY	N	359	5	9	18394
Abel, Sarah	12-Apr-76	04-Nov-52	W	F	Cytotechnician	MEDICAL LABORATORY	N	342	4	9	15723

SALARY	BENEFITS	PERCENTAGE
$36,983.00	$4,093.00	
$54,159.00	$4,093.00	
$17,815.00	$4,093.00	
$16,234.00	$4,093.00	
$24,199.00	$4,093.00	
$19,587.00	$4,093.00	

Criterion

SALARY	BENEFITS	PERCENTAGE
36983		

These subcommands are presented since Lotus 1-2-3 found that a file called TUTOR already exists on the Working Diskette. You can write over the old version of TUTOR by typing R (REPLACE). Again, Lotus 1-2-3 will flash the word WAIT as it replaces the old version of TUTOR with the active file in which you wrote your name.

Protected Cells

With the modified active file of TUTOR still visible on the computer screen, you will notice another important characteristic of this and other files from the HR Data Diskette. Move the cursor to cell A1 (press the Home key), and try to type anything such as your name. Then press the Enter key. Lotus 1-2-3 will beep, and it will flash the message **ERROR** in the upper right of the screen. It will also show the words "Protected cell" in the lower left of the screen. Press the Escape key, and Lotus 1-2-3 will return to the Ready mode without having altered the contents of cell A1.

Certain cells of selected files are protected in order to prevent you from making errors. You may disable the protection by typing the following:

/WGPD (WORKSHEET GLOBAL PROTECTION DISABLE)

Generally you will want to leave a file protected since the protection will prevent your accidentally erasing or writing over information that you need in order to complete the analyses called for by a given chapter of this book.

Printing the Worksheets

The /P (PRINT) command is used to print a worksheet. Before using this command, verify that the printer which is connected to your computer is turned on and is on line (i.e., ready to receive information from the computer). You will also want to adjust the paper so that the top of a page is aligned correctly for the printer. If you do not have the HR Data Diskette file called TUTOR as your active file, retrieve it from the HR Data Diskette. Make sure that the cursor is at cell A1 before using the Print commands. You can press the Home key to move the cursor to A1.

Typing /P (PRINT) causes the following commands to be written at the top of the screen:

Printer   File

Select the Printer command by typing P (PRINTER). You will then see the following subcommands at the top of the screen:

Range   Line   Page   Options   Clear   Align   Go   Quit

Type R (RANGE) to let Lotus 1-2-3 know which section of the work-

sheet you want to print. Lotus 1-2-3 will respond with the following
prompt:

Enter Print range: A1

You must now define the **coordinates** (the area of the worksheet) of
the worksheet block that you want to print. In most cases, the upper left
coordinate will be A1. Therefore, type A1; then type a period. Then provide Lotus 1-2-3 with the cell address or coordinate of the lower right
corner of the block. Use E16 as the lower right corner. Type this cell address and press the Enter key. The Print submenu will reappear, and the
print range will have been stored.

Verify that this range is stored by typing R (RANGE) once again. You
will see that the area bounded by A1 and E16 is highlighted. Be sure to
press the Enter key again to verify that this is the range you want to
print. Pressing any other key will change the range.

Typing AG (ALIGN GO) causes Lotus 1-2-3 to reset to the top of the
page of the paper in the printer and begin printing at that point. If you
type AG (ALIGN GO) but your printer fails to work, your printer may not be
turned on or it may not be ready. Correct the problem with the printer;
then type AG (ALIGN GO). With some versions of Lotus 1-2-3, you may have
to press the Escape key before proceeding to print the range you identified within the file TUTOR.

While printing, Lotus 1-2-3 will flash the word **WAIT** in the upper
right corner of the screen. After completing the printing, Lotus 1-2-3
will return to the Print commands. To leave the Print commands, type Q
(QUIT). This Quit command does not quit Lotus 1-2-3; instead, it leaves
one of the Lotus 1-2-3 menus--the Print command menu.

Lotus 1-2-3 Commands for Data Management

Large databases contain many records with many fields per record. In
a HR database, each record represents an employee or applicant for employment; it is a row of data on the Lotus 1-2-3 worksheet. Each field
represents a topic or type of information in a separate column. For example, a field can be the department in which each employee works.

With many records and many fields, it becomes very difficult to find
a single employee or groups of employees with certain characteristics. For
example, you may be interested in finding all of the employees whose
salaries are within some range. You could scroll thru the data in order to
find all employees whose salaries are between $15,000 and $23,000, but
this laborious activity is unnecessary. There are two data management
functions that Lotus 1-2-3 provides to help you in finding these employees: the Sort command and the Query command.

The Sort Command. The Sort command is a Lotus 1-2-3 subcommand of
the Data command. It allows you to reorganize data. Thus, you can reorder
the employee records by salary so that all employees whose salaries are

between $15,000 and $23,000 are immediately adjacent to one another.

Before learning how to use the Lotus 1-2-3 Sort command, retrieve the file called TUTOR if you are not already working with it. When Lotus 1-2-3 returns to the Ready mode, move the cursor down until rows 21-27 are visible on the screen. You should see the following data and labels:

	A	B	C
21	SALARY	BENEFITS	PERCENTAGE
22	$36,983.00	$4,093.00	
23	$54,159.00	$4,093.00	
24	$17,815.00	$4,093.00	
25	$16,234.00	$4,093.00	
26	$24,199.00	$4,093.00	
27	$19,587.00	$4,093.00	

Now access the Sort command by typing /DS (DATA SORT). As you can see at the top of the screen, the Sort commands include the following:

Data-Range   Primary-Key   Secondary-Key   Reset   Go   Quit

The steps in sorting data include defining the range of data to be sorted. With the Sort command menu visible at the top of the screen, type D (DATA-RANGE), and Lotus 1-2-3 will prompt with the following:

Enter Data-Range:

At this prompt, enter the coordinates from the area you wish to sort. This area should include all rows and columns containing data within the database. In this case, the response to the Lotus 1-2-3 prompt for a Data-Range is:

A22..B27

The range should not include the field names which one typically finds at the top of each column of data. As is the case in establishing a print range, the coordinates are cell addresses of the upper left cell and the lower right cell of the area of the database. After entering the coordinates A22..B27, press the Enter key to store the range of data to be sorted. You must now choose the field or column on which the sort will be based. Type P (PRIMARY-KEY) to produce the following prompt:

Enter Primary sort key address:

At this prompt, enter the address of the first entry in the column of data (within the data range) which is to form the basis of the sort. For example, if you wish to sort by salary the data in A22..B27 of the file TUTOR, A22 is the cell address with which you respond to the Lotus 1-2-3 prompt.

Immediately following the entry of the cell address, Lotus 1-2-3 prompts with the following:

Enter Primary sort key address: A22 Enter Sort order (A or D):

The sort order may be ascending (A) or descending (D). Let us assume that you wish the salaries to ascend from lowest to highest. Therefore, enter A unless Lotus 1-2-3 already shows an A after the colon. Then press the Enter key. Lotus 1-2-3 will then produce the same Sort command menu that you have seen before. Selecting and typing G (GO) will initiate the sort. The resulting reorganization of the data in the worksheet area of A22..B27 should be as follows:

	A	B	C
21	SALARY	BENEFITS	PERCENTAGE
22	$16,234.00	$4,093.00	
23	$17,815.00	$4,093.00	
24	$19,587.00	$4,093.00	
25	$24,199.00	$4,093.00	
26	$36,983.00	$4,093.00	
27	$54,159.00	$4,093.00	

Your instructor may direct you to print the sorted table. If so, the print range should be A1..B27. (For additional help in printing these results, you may wish to return to the section on Printing the Worksheets in this chapter.)

The Database Query Command. Sometimes sorting the database is not the easiest way to isolate the information within the database in which you are interested. Lotus 1-2-3 provides a series of query subcommands that may be used to extract cases from a database. These commands require that you create a database. Actually, the database has already been created in that the data and the field names are already there. However, someone must tell Lotus 1-2-3 the names of the fields and the area of the worksheet in which the database is located. This is the meaning of "create a database."

Before proceeding with this section of the chapter, retrieve the file called TUTOR from the HR Database Diskette if you are not already working with this file. With Lotus 1-2-3 in the Ready mode, scroll down from A1 until rows 21-40 are visible on the screen.

The database commands are accessed by typing /DQ (DATA QUERY). These commands produce the following menu:

Input Criterion Output Find Extract Unique Delete Reset Quit

Input, Criterion, and Output are setup commands that establish the parameters of the database for Lotus 1-2-3. The Input command lets Lotus 1-2-3 know in what part of the worksheet the database is located. The Criterion command establishes the question or query upon which the database search is based. The Output command establishes the area of the worksheet into which cases that are extracted from the database will be writ-

23

ten.

Extract, Unique, and Delete are commands that isolate the cases which match the criterion. With this book you will only have to use the Extract command for the assignments.

The Reset command erases the information that is stored for the three setup commands, and the Quit command leaves this set of Lotus 1-2-3 subcommands. The Reset command does not erase the information in your active file, nor does the Quit command from the Query command menu result in your leaving Lotus 1-2-3.

In using a database, the first step is to establish the input range of the worksheet area which makes up the database. If the Data Query command menu is visible at the top of the screen, type I (INPUT). If not, type /DQI (DATA QUERY INPUT). Lotus 1-2-3 will respond with the following prompt:

Enter Input range:

At this prompt you will normally enter the cell coordinates that define the area of the worksheet. Since these have already been entered and stored, you will observe that the worksheet area of A21..C27 is highlighted. Notice that the upper left coordinate of the input area must include the row (containing the field names) just above the first data entry. Including the field names in the input area is essential since questions directed to Lotus 1-2-3 about the database will be phrased in terms of the data associated with these field names. Press the Enter key to verify that this is the worksheet area which forms the input area of the database. Then Lotus 1-2-3 will provide the data query command menu which you have seen before.

The next step is to specify a criterion upon which a search of the database can be made. This criterion consists of two parts: the field name and the specific basis of the search. Thus, a criterion range must encompass at least two rows of the worksheet. Type C (CRITERION) and Lotus 1-2-3 will respond with the following prompt:

Enter Criterion range:

Normally you must type in the criterion range. In this example, it is already stored as A31..A32. Notice that the criterion includes the field name Salary and a value 36983 from the database. You should also notice that care was taken to enter the word Salary just as it appears in the database. Press the Enter key in order to verify this range, for the criteria must exactly match the field being searched.

The last task in "creating a database" is to establish an area of the worksheet in which to write the extracted cases. With the data query command menu visible, type O (OUTPUT), and Lotus 1-2-3 will prompt with the following:

Enter Output range:

The range for the output is A36..C39. An output range must contain at least two rows of the worksheet for essentially the same reason you had to identify two rows in establishing the criterion. One row must contain the names of the fields, and at least one row must be provided for the data that will be extracted from the database. The number of rows which are stored as the output range depends on the number of cases that are to be extracted. If you fail to enter a range with enough rows, Lotus 1-2-3 will fill the range that you have identified and provide an error message stating that there were too many cases for the established range. After having reviewed the output range, press the Enter key.

Having completed the creation of the database, you may now extract data which match the established criterion. Lotus 1-2-3 permits you to extract data if you type E (EXTRACT) as long as the DQ (DATA QUERY) commands are still visible at the top of the screen. You will observe that records for which there is a salary of 36983 are written into the output area of the worksheet. You may now quit the data query command menu by typing Q (QUIT). Your instructor may direct that you print these results. If so, use A1..C39 as the print range.

Conclusion

Now that you have read this chapter and performed the brief "practice" exercises in it, you should have a basic understanding of some of the capabilities of Lotus 1-2-3. This chapter was not designed to cover all of the aspects of Lotus 1-2-3, nor was it designed to provide an in-depth understanding of Lotus 1-2-3.

Remember that the early chapters of this book will assume only that you have read this chapter. Thus, they will provide step-by-step instructions of the commands that are required for the analyses. Naturally, later chapters of this book will assume that you have gained some expertise in using Lotus 1-2-3, and some procedures will no longer be explained in the detail found in this and early chapters that contain HR exercises. Should you find yourself unable to complete a procedure for which the specific steps are not outlined in later chapters, consult this chapter.

If, after reading this introduction, you find that you need more practice with Lotus 1-2-3 before beginning the subsequent chapters that contain Lotus 1-2-3 exercises, you should turn to the following:

1. Lotus 1-2-3 Tutorial disk that comes with the Lotus 1-2-3 software.
2. The <u>Reference Manual</u>[1] published by Lotus 1-2-3.
3. <u>Lotus 1-2-3 Quick</u> by Gaylord N. Smith.[2]

There are also many Lotus 1-2-3 guides that are available in most bookstores. Working your way through the Lotus 1-2-3 Tutorial disk or consulting one of the written guides will provide you with additional skill in using Lotus 1-2-3, and it will allay normal anxiety that is associated with the first-time use of an electronic spreadsheet.

Endnotes

1. Reference Manual (Cambridge, MA: Lotus Development Corporation, 1985).
2. Gaylord N. Smith, Lotus 1-2-3 Quick (Cincinnati: South-Western Publishing Co., 1986).

CHAPTER 3
THE ENVIRONMENT FOR HUMAN RESOURCES MANAGEMENT

Lotus 1-2-3 applications in this chapter (all of these Lotus 1-2-3 applications are explained in Chapter 2):

Command Menus
  FILE
  PRINT
  DATA QUERY
Mathematical Operations
  Multiplication
  Subtraction
Statistical Functions
  @COUNT
  @SUM

Chapter Outline

Organizations that do not <u>anticipate</u> changes in their environments must <u>adapt</u> to changes. Whether anticipated or not, change is inevitable. HR departments, like any other area of an organization, must respond to the rapidly occurring changes in their environments.

Among the many environmentally induced changes in human resources management (HRM) is the addition of a large number of women to the work force. While this addition alone represents changing demands on the HR functions, the particular sociodemographic characteristics of the additional women add other demands to the management of human resources.

Among those sociodemographic characteristics are the changing number of women in their child-bearing years who enter and remain in the work force. More and more women with preschool children and elementary school children are working full time for a variety of reasons. Women have delayed pregnancies until they are older; thus, more women have participated in the work force a longer period of time prior to the first pregnancy and they find themselves well established in their careers. Moreover, the family unit finds itself accustomed to the income of both spouses. Still other women face raising children alone without an option to their continued work force participation.

The result of these changes in the American labor force has been a change in the demand for preschool and after-school child care. Whereas extended families may have stepped in to provide child care in another era, today women find themselves with few alternatives to organized day care. Unfortunately this option is not entirely satisfactory. It is costly. It frequently is inconvenient relative to the workplace, and it leaves unresolved the anxiety about a child who becomes sick at some distance from a parent's workplace.

As a result of such shortcomings associated with day care, many organizations have begun to consider their own day-care operations. While this option incurs costs and liabilities for the business, it brings several advantages. Absenteeism and tardiness are reduced as a result of the ease with which employees may both take their children to day care and come to work. Stress may be reduced as well since the children are located close by and the employees may more easily deal with illnesses or related problems that occur over the course of the workday. Moreover, the reduced problems associated with commuting to two locations in the morning may reduce stress.

Background of the Exercise

As a consequence of these advantages, its concern for its employees, and the growing trend in American business to provide day-care facilities, Metro Hospital has decided to evaluate the need and costs for day-care facilities for its employees. Its approach to the evaluation was to survey its employees to determine the demand and the willingness of employees to pay various amounts per month per child for day care. From information it has gathered separately, the HR Department of Metro Hospital estimates that the cost per child per month is about $175. This cost will provide a day-care experience which includes some organized educational activities, lunch, and snacks. Facilities will be donated by the hospital.

The goals of the staff of the HR Department are to (1) determine the extent of interest in day-care facilities on the work premises, and (2) evaluate the cost of providing these facilities. A questionnaire was sent to all employees, and the return rate was very high. Since the responses were not anonymous, they were temporarily stored with other information in the HR Database.

Retrieving CHILD

To aid the staff in accomplishing its goals, you will analyze the demand for and costs of providing child care. Place your HR Data Diskette in drive A and retrieve the file called CHILD. You must already have loaded Lotus 1-2-3 to be able to retrieve CHILD. (If you are having difficulty in loading Lotus 1-2-3, review the section on Getting Started in

Chapter 2. You may also want to seek the assistance of the computer
laboratory assistant or your instructor.)

Once you see the Lotus 1-2-3 screen with the cell column letters
across the top of the screen and the cell row numbers to the left, you are
ready to retrieve CHILD. Type /FR (FILE RETRIEVE). When the filenames from
the HR Data Diskette appear, move the cursor to the right until the file
CHILD is highlighted. Press the Enter key. (Additional information is
available from the section on Saving and Retrieving Files in Chapter 2.)

As soon as Lotus 1-2-3 has loaded the file CHILD from the HR Data
Diskette, you will see a screen similar to the one displayed in Exhibit
3-1. Before continuing with this chapter, remove the HR Data Diskette from
your computer's drive and replace it with the formatted diskette on which
you stored TUTOR from Chapter 2. You will store your work from this chapter onto the Working Diskette rather than the HR Data Diskette. This is
the procedure you will follow in all subsequent chapters.

Four-Part Output Screen

There are four output screens in this exercise (see Exhibits 3-1a
and 3-1b). In cells A5..F23 is Output Screen 1, which must be completed
and turned in to your instructor. In cell A1 is the name of the file that
you retrieved from the HR Data Diskette. In cell A2 is the name of this
exercise, and cell A3 provides a space for typing your own name.

Begin each exercise by typing your name in cell A3. An easy way to
do this is to move the cursor to cell A3 and press the F2 key. The F2 key
puts Lotus 1-2-3 in the Edit mode. In the Edit mode, you can type your
name to the right of the word **Name:**. After typing your name and pressing
the Return key, Lotus 1-2-3 will return to the Ready mode.

Cells A6..F13 contain the output of the database queries. All of
these cells are protected; the values are automatically transferred from
another part of the worksheet.

There are four columns in Output Screen 1. Column A identifies the
output based on responses to the questionnaire. Column B is a simple
count of the number of respondents who fell into each of the categories
from column A. Column D is a sum of the number of children under age 7 as
reported by each respondent. Column F is the cumulative sum, for example:

+F9+D10

Exhibit 3-1a

CHILD
The Environment For Human Resources Management
Name:

OUTPUT SCREEN 1

Data Base Query	Count	Number of Children	Cumulative Number
Pay More Than $200	0	0	0
Pay $100-$200	0	0	0
Pay Less Than $100	0	0	0
Will Not Use	36	-	
Use Day Care	36	43	

	Monthly	Yearly
Revenue @ Price of $99	$0	$0
Expense @ Price of $99	$0	$0
Profit/Loss	$0	$0
Revenue @ Price of $199	$0	$0
Expense @ Price of $199	$0	$0
Profit/Loss	$0	$0

OUTPUT SCREEN 2
Pay Less Than $100
CRITERION

NAME	AGE	SEX	BELOW 7	USE	PAY
					1

QUERY OUTPUT

NAME	AGE	SEX	BELOW 7	USE	PAY

TOTAL COUNT	0
NUMBER OF CHILDREN	0

Exhibit 3-1b

OUTPUT SCREEN 3
Pay $100-$200
CRITERION

NAME	AGE	SEX	BELOW 7	USE	PAY
					0

QUERY OUTPUT

NAME	AGE	SEX	BELOW 7	USE	PAY

TOTAL COUNT	0
NUMBER OF CHILDREN	0

OUTPUT SCREEN 4
Pay More Than $200
CRITERION

NAME	AGE	SEX	BELOW 7	USE	PAY
					0

QUERY OUTPUT

NAME	AGE	SEX	BELOW 7	USE	PAY

TOTAL COUNT	0
NUMBER OF CHILDREN	0

Cells A17..F23 contain the calculations of the cost of the day care for Metro Hospital. You will notice that some cells are protected and others are unprotected. If you have a color monitor, the values in cells D21..D23 are green; they are highlighted if you have a monochrome monitor. The green color (or highlighting) indicates that the cells are un-protected. In this chapter, these are cells in which you must supply some information before turning in the assignment. In subsequent chapters, you will find that green or highlighted cells of an output screen require that you supply information.

Output Screens 2, 3, and 4 are located in cells A26..F87. From the green characters (or highlighted characters on a monochrome screen), you can see that there is information which you must supply. Output Screen 2, beginning at cell A26, is provided for extracting the respondents to the survey who are willing to pay less than $100. Output Screen 3 is designed to obtain information about those who are willing to pay from $100 to $200, and Output Screen 4 is designed to obtain information about those who are willing to pay more than $200.

Input Screen

In each exercise there will be a portion of the HR Database from Metro Hospital. Since you are usually only interested in some of the fields (e.g., race or salary or performance scores), you will see only a limited number of the fields from the entire database. Think of this slice of the database as the part which some staff member selected for the par-ticular HR problem under study. As you complete more of the exercises in this book, you will become familiar with the database and you will observe that the slice which you see in any given chapter is a part of the larger database.

The slice of the database that you will use will be located below or to the right and below the output screen. For this exercise, the selected database fields are located in cells A90..F127.

Move the cursor to cell A90. An easy way to move the cursor is to press F5, the function key labeled "GoTo." Then Lotus 1-2-3 will display the following prompt at the top of the screen:

Enter address to go to:

The cell address for the cell at which your cursor is located at the time you press F5 will also appear at the top of the screen after the colon. Type the cell address (e.g., A90) to which you wish to move the cursor and press the Enter key. Lotus 1-2-3 will move the cursor to this new location.

In cell A90 is the word DATABASE. Below it are the fields which were selected from the larger HR Database for this exercise. In this case, you will observe that the following fields were selected: Name, Age, Below 7,

Use, and Pay. The last three fields represent responses to the questionnaire that the HR Department sent to all employees of Metro Hospital. Those fields represent the following questions:

1. How many children do you have below 7? (Below 7)
2. Do you use a day-care facility in caring for your children? (Use)
3. How much would you be willing to pay per month per child for day care if facilities were operated by Metro Hospital? (Pay)

Responses to the "Below 7" question represent the number of children. Responses to the "Use" question are Y for Yes or N for No, and responses to the "Pay" question are coded as follows:

1 = <u>Willing to pay less than $100 per child per month</u>
2 = <u>Willing to pay $100-200 per child per month</u>
3 = <u>Willing to pay more than $200 per child per month</u>
4 = <u>No response to this question or unwilling to state</u>
<u>an amount</u>

Below the HR Database in cells A128..D129 is summary information about the respondents. This slice of the HR Database contains only employees who indicated that they have at least one child below 7 for whom they use day care. A count of the number of respondents who met these restrictions is contained in cell D128. The following formula was used:

@COUNT(E92..E127)

This statistical function counts the number of entries in the area specified within the parentheses.

The formula below adds the number of children below 7 years old whom these 36 employees reported having and are now in day care:

@SUM(D92..D127)

Notice that the same area of the worksheet is specified within the parentheses; however, the statistical function for summing <u>adds</u> the entries rather than counting them.

Analysis

With the information that you now have about the output screens and the input screen (the database), you can begin the analyses required by this exercise.

Output Screen 1. Return to Output Screen 1 at cell A5. (Instead of using the "GoTo" method with the F5 key, you can press the Home key to return the cursor to cell A1.) Review this screen in light of your goals: (1) to determine the extent of interest in day-care facilities on the work premises, and (2) to evaluate the cost of providing these facilities. In other words, you must count the number of employees interested in the various options based on varied prices and calculate the expense of each of these options. To accomplish these goals and complete Output Screen 1, you will need to extract information from the HR Database (the input screen).

Output Screen 2. Output Screen 2 at cell A26 is provided for extracting the respondents to the survey who are willing to pay less than $100. To extract these respondents, use the Data Query command menu. With the cursor in cell A26, type /DQ (DATA QUERY). This command menu allows you to "create the database" and extract data from it. (You may wish to review the subsection on the Database Query Command in Chapter 2.)

Begin by creating the database, i.e., establishing the parameters of the database. Type I (INPUT) to establish the area of the database from which you will make a selection of some part of the data. Move the cursor to cell A91. This is the first actual cell of this slice of the HR Database. Type a period and move the cursor to F91. Now move the cursor down to cell F127. The entire area of the database, including the field names, is now highlighted. Press the Enter key. Remember that it is important to include the field names as well as the data themselves in the input area of the database.

Now you are ready to establish a criterion for extracting data from the database. The first criterion is to identify those employees who will pay less than $100. Type C (CRITERION) and move the cursor to F29. Type a period and move the cursor to F30, highlighting cells F29..F30. Press the Enter key to store the criterion.

Notice that there is only one entry in row 30 which is a part of this criterion. That entry is a 1 (one) beneath the field name Pay. The criterion which you have established will select respondents who are willing to pay less than $100. Recall that the field name Pay refers to the question from the employee questionnaire: "How much would you be willing to pay per month per child for day care if facilities were operated by Metro Hospital?" The code, 1, represents "Willing to pay less than $100 per child per month."

You are now ready to establish an area of the worksheet in which to write the data that you will extract from the database. At the Data Query menu, type O (OUTPUT). Move the cursor to cell A32, type a period, move the cursor across to F32, and then move it down to F48. This area represents the output area. Press the Enter key to store this output area.

Once you have established the output area, you can extract a portion of your database. Notice that cells A32..F32 (within the output area) contain fields from the input area that you established earlier. In extracting data from the database, you will obtain field information which corresponds to each of these fields in cells A32..F32 for every employee who has a value of 1 in the Pay column of the database. To extract this information from the database, type E (EXTRACT). To return Lotus 1-2-3 to the Ready mode, type Q (QUIT).

34

With Lotus 1-2-3 in the Ready mode (without a menu at the top of the screen), move the cursor to cell D49. You are now ready to supply two pieces of information that are required in Output Screen 1: (1) a count of the number of employees who are willing to pay less than $100 per child for child care, and (2) the number of children of employees in this group. At cell D49, enter the following statistical function for counting the employees:

@COUNT(E92..E127)

Next, enter the statistical function @SUM in cell D50 to add the number of children of employees in this group. This statistical function will take the following form:

@SUM (D92..D127)

Move the cursor to cell A1 and review the changes that have occurred in Output Screen 1. You now know the number of employees who are willing to pay an amount less than $100 and how many children of day-care age these employees have.

As you can see, there is still additional information which you must obtain in order to complete Output Screen 1. You will need information about employees who are willing to pay between $100 and $200 per child per month for day care, and you need information about those who are willing to pay more than $200.

Output Screen 3. Output Screen 3 (cell A53) already has the field names listed for the criterion and the output areas for extracting the employees who are willing to pay between $100 and $200 per month per child. Go to cell F57 and enter a 2--the code for this group. (Cell F57 is just below the field name, Pay.)

You are now ready to create the database and extract the data which matches the criterion. Type /DQ (DATA QUERY). Since Lotus 1-2-3 still has stored the database parameters that you used to extract data about those employees who would pay less than $100, you will have to erase these settings. Type R (RESET); now you are prepared to follow the steps you used in extracting data for employees who were willing to pay less than $100 per month per child. In this instance, you will extract data about those employees who are willing to pay between $100 and $200.

Next, type I (Input) and move the cursor to the first cell of the database. Remember that the first cell is the cell containing the field name just above the first piece of data in the upper left corner of a database. Highlight the entire database, A91..F127, and press the Enter key. Then type C (CRITERION) and highlight the field name Pay, as well as the code, 2 (cells F56..F57). Press Enter and type O (OUTPUT). Highlight the area, A59..F71 and press the Enter key. Then type E (EXTRACT). When the Data Query command menu returns to the top of the screen, you may quit this command menu and return to the Ready mode by typing Q (QUIT).

To provide the requested information in Output Screen 1 about the group of employees who will pay from $100 to $200 for child care, use the statistical function @COUNT in cell D72. With this function you can count the number of employees in the worksheet area D60..D71. This number is the TOTAL COUNT referred to in cell A72.

Next, calculate the number of children of child-care age. Cell A73 with its entry, NUMBER OF CHILDREN, refers to the required entry in cell D73. Since you must add the number of children in this column, you will need the statistical function @SUM to add the entries in the worksheet area from D60 to D71. Enter the appropriate form of the statistical function @SUM in cell D73. If you wish, you may return to Output Screen 1 to verify that the information you just obtained has been entered in the correct cells of this output screen.

Output Screen 4. Output Screen 4 is located in cells A76..F87. From this output screen, you will obtain information about those employees who are willing to pay more than $200 per child for child care. The code for this group of employees is 3. Begin your work with Output Screen 4 by completing the criterion. In row 80, enter the code 3 below the field name Pay.

To reset the settings for each of the database parameters, type /DQR (DATA QUERY RESET). Proceed to establish the input area (A91..F127), the output area (A82..F85), and the criterion area (F79..F80). Then extract information about the employees who are willing to pay more than $200 per month per child for child care. Return to the Ready mode of Lotus 1-2-3 by quitting the menu. Now you may enter the statistical functions in cells D86 and D87 which provide the Total Count of employees who will pay more than $200 and the number of children of employees in this group.

Return the cursor to cell A1. Cells B9..F13 should now be complete. You have obtained the necessary information for making judgments about the interest in child care at Metro Hospital, but you still do not have information about the cost of providing this service.

Assumptions. Cells A17 to F19 provide output space for calculating the expenses and revenue if a price of $99 per month per child is adopted. To complete these calculations, you must assume that all persons who said they were interested in day care at Metro Hospital for this price will actually place their children at Metro's day-care center. For the sake of this analysis, also assume that those who say they will pay more than $100 will pay less than that amount.

Formulas. The required formula in cell D17 multiplies the $99 monthly price by the total number of children whose parents will pay $99. The formula looks like this:

+F11*99

The number in cell F11 is the cumulative number of children whose parents will pay a certain amount or more. Note the formula which was used for calculating F11. It adds the number of children from parents who will pay no more than $99 to the number of children whose parents will pay some amount greater than $99. Since the staff found that it can provide the service for a cost of $175 per child per month, the entry in cell D18 is:

+F11*175

The profit or loss is the remainder from subtracting the expense from the revenue. Thus, the entry in cell D19 is:

+D17-D18

Yearly revenue and expense are calculated by multiplying the values in column F by 12. Thus, the yearly revenue for the $99 per month price may be calculated by entering the following formula in cell F17:

+D17*12

A similar formula may be used for calculating the yearly expense. This formula should be typed into cell F18. The yearly profit or loss is calculated just like the monthly profit or loss, using cells from column F in the formula. You should not multiply the profit/loss in cell D19 by 12. Instead, you should subtract the yearly expense (F18) from the yearly revenue (F17). As you can now see, the yearly loss will be $32,832. Using this example, create formulas in cells D21..D23 and cells F21..F23 to calculate the loss or gain associated with charging employees a price of $199 per month per child. To multiply by the appropriate number of children, use data in the column labeled Cumulative Number—column F (cells F6..F12).

Saving Your Worksheets

To save your work, type /FS (FILE SAVE). Lotus 1-2-3 will respond with the name of the file on which you are working, CHILD. Press the Enter key to indicate that this name is the one under which you wish to save the current worksheet. Since you replaced the HR Data Diskette with the Working Diskette, Lotus 1-2-3 will proceed to save this file under the name CHILD on the Working Diskette. If you subsequently retrieve CHILD from the Working Diskette and then save it, Lotus 1-2-3 will respond with the following prompts:

Cancel   Replace

Type R (REPLACE), and Lotus 1-2-3 will write the changes you have made over the old file on the Working Diskette.

Printing the Results

Return to cell A1 on the Lotus 1-2-3 worksheet. Make sure that you have typed your name after the word **Name:** in cell A3. To access the Lotus 1-2-3 print menu of commands, type /PP (PRINT PRINTER). Then type R (RANGE). Notice that the print range of A1..F23 is highlighted, and this range is entered at the top of your screen:

Enter Print range: A1..F23

Press the Enter key to indicate that this is the range you wish to print. Check to see that your printer is ready and the paper is aligned correctly with the top of the page of paper as the first line to be printed. Now type AG (ALIGN GO). These commands will cause Lotus 1-2-3 to treat the current page position in your printer as the top of the page, and printing will begin. After the printer stops, type P (PAGE) to advance to the top of the next page of paper in your printer. To leave the Lotus 1-2-3 Print menu, type Q (QUIT).

Analyzing the Results

You are now ready to use the information that you have obtained from the HR Database in order to make some decisions. In the space provided, answer the questions at the end of this chapter. Then tear out that page, attach it to the printed results, and turn in both items to your instructor.

Questions

1. To what degree is the interest of employees in day care affected by the price of day care?

2. Evaluate whether it is reasonable to assume that those who are willing to pay more than $99 will pay this low price for day care.

3. What do you recommend that Metro Hospital do about providing child-care facilities? Include your price recommendation if you recommend this option.

4. What other alternatives might Metro Hospital pursue in order to reduce the costs of day care yet provide it to employees who wish it?

CHAPTER 4
EQUAL EMPLOYMENT OPPORTUNITY AND AFFIRMATIVE ACTION:
THE EEO-1 REPORT

Lotus 1-2-3 applications in this chapter:

Command Menus
    FILE
    PRINT
    DATA QUERY
    COPY*
Statistical Functions
    @COUNT
    @SUM
Database Statistical Function
    @DCOUNT*

Chapter Outline

Background of the Exercise
Retrieving EEO1
Output Screen
Database Statistical Function: @DCOUNT
Input Screen
Analysis
    Counting the Number of Black Males
    Building the Utilization Table
Saving Your Worksheets
Printing the Results
Analyzing the Results

There is substantial legal justification for United States companies to comply with the laws and regulations associated with equal employment opportunity and affirmative action. Of course, there are also ethical reasons that warrant an organization's concern for its employment practices.

These employment practices affect the selection of women and minority employees and their job assignments and rewards. To comply with the law and establish policies designed to provide affirmative action for women and minority employees, an organization must know how many of its employees fall into each of the affected classes, or **protected classes**, that the United States government has identified. Those protected classes include females and members of the following ethnic and racial groups: Asians, Blacks, Native Americans, and persons of Hispanic origin. To determine the number of employees in each of these categories, companies complete a **utilization analysis**, which merely refers to a count of its employees by sex and racial classification.

_____
*Indicates a first-time use of this Lotus 1-2-3 application in this book.

41

An organization may use its utilization analysis for a variety of purposes. From these data, an organization files its required EEO-1 report. A utilization analysis also forms the basis for the development of an affirmative action plan. Other typical uses of a utilization analysis include an evaluation of the impact of a reduction in force (a layoff). This chapter will guide you in completing a utilization analysis from which the data may be entered in an EEO-1 report.

Background of the Exercise

Not surprisingly, a HR database offers the user a substantial advantage in completing a utilization analysis. Since the data are already stored in association with fields for race and sex, the objective is more easily accomplished. A user only has to pose a database query that will result in counting the number of employees in each category. Since the staff of Metro Hospital's HR Department must complete its EEO-1 report, your task is to provide the information necessary to complete this report. That is, you must build the table which the staff will use in obtaining this information from year to year. You also will want to evaluate the hospital's distribution of employees by sex and racial group.

Retrieving EEO1

To retrieve the file called EEO1 from your HR Data Diskette, you must have already loaded Lotus 1-2-3. (If you are having difficulty in loading Lotus 1-2-3, review the section on Getting Started in Chapter 2. You may also need to seek the assistance of the computer laboratory assistant or your instructor.)

Once you see the Lotus 1-2-3 screen with the cell column letters across the top of the screen and the cell row numbers to the left, you are ready to retrieve EEO1. Type /FR. Move the cursor to the right until the file EEO1 is highlighted. Press the Enter key. As soon as you see that Lotus 1-2-3 has loaded EEO1, remove the HR Data Diskette from your computer's drive and replace it with the formatted Working Diskette on which you have stored TUTOR from Chapter 2 and CHILD from Chapter 3. You will store your work from this chapter and subsequent chapters on this Working Diskette rather than on the HR Data Diskette.

Output Screen

In cells A1..G32 is the output screen (see Exhibit 4-1) which must be completed and turned in to your instructor. Observe that cell A1 contains the name of this Lotus 1-2-3 file. Cell A2 contains the subtitle of this chapter, which is the name of this exercise. Cell A3 provides a space for your name. Begin by typing your name after the word **Name:**. You can do this by moving the cursor to cell A3 and pressing the F2 key (the edit function key). Type your name; then press the Enter key.

Exhibit 4-1

EEO1
Equal Employment Opportunity and Affirmative Action: The EEO-1
Name:

OUTPUT SCREEN

```
                           CRITERION
                           RACE  SEX
                            B     M

          NAME            RACE  SEX
```

COUNT FROM DATA EXTRACTION   =   0

UTILIZATION TABLE

RACE	SEX			PERCENTAGES		
	FEMALE	MALE	SUM	FEMALE	MALE	TOTAL
ASIAN	0	0	0	0.0%	0.0%	0.0%
BLACK	0	4	0	0.0%	0.0%	0.0%
NATIVE AMERICAN	0	0	0	0.0%	0.0%	0.0%
HISPANIC ORIGIN	0	0	0	0.0%	0.0%	0.0%
WHITE, NON HISPANIC	0	0	0	0.0%	0.0%	0.0%
TOTALS	0	0	0	0.0%	0.0%	0.0%

The first portion of the output screen is located in cells A6..D15 and uses the database features of Lotus 1-2-3 to extract information about one of the EEO1 categories: Black males. This portion contains the criterion and field names for the data output of employees who are Black males. It also requests that you use the statistical function @COUNT to count the number of employees who are extracted from the HR Database.

The second portion of the output screen is a utilization table which is located in cells A17..G32. This table allows you to count the number of persons in each EEO category and then calculate the percentage of the total number of employees represented by this EEO category.

Database Statistical Function @DCOUNT

You will learn to use a database statistical function in this chapter. In learning to use this database statistical function, it will probably help to first see how the database query Extract command and the statistical function @COUNT (both of which were explained in Chapter 2) provide the same information as the database statistical function @DCOUNT. Therefore, complete the first portion of the output screen as a demonstration of the use of the Extract command and the statistical function @COUNT.

The database statistical function @DCOUNT is introduced to show how it permits you to obtain the same information as the Extract command without providing an output area of the worksheet for the extracted cases. It will also allow you to construct a table that may be used time after time to obtain utilization information about a changing work force.

Input Screen

The slice of the database that you will use will be located below or to the right and below the output screen. For this exercise the selected database fields are located in cells H36..L158.

Move the cursor to cell H36. An easy way to move the cursor is to press F5, the function key labeled GoTo. Lotus 1-2-3 will then display the following at the top of the screen:

Enter address to go to:

The cell address for the cell at which your cursor is located at the time you press F5 will also appear at the top of the screen after the colon. Then type the cell address (e.g., H36) to which you wish to move the cursor and press the Enter key. Lotus 1-2-3 will move the cursor to this new location.

In cell H36 is the word DATABASE. Below it are the fields that were extracted from the larger HR database for this exercise: Name (of the employee), Race, Sex, Job Title, and Department.

Analysis

With the information that you now have about the output screen and the input screen (the database), you can begin the analyses required by this exercise. Return to cell A1. You can do this by pressing F5 (function key 5) and entering A1 when Lotus 1-2-3 prompts with the following:

Enter address to go to:

or you can press the Home key.

Counting the Number of Black Males. Your first task is to count the number of Black males in this slice of the HR Database by extracting all employees whose race is Black and whose sex is male. To accomplish this task, you will have to "create a database." In other words, you will have to establish the parameters for the database. To access the Lotus 1-2-3 commands associated with database queries, type /DQ (DATA QUERY). Then type I (INPUT) and observe that the input range for the database (H37..L158) has already been established. Therefore, this area of the worksheet is highlighted on your screen. Press the Enter key to confirm for Lotus 1-2-3 that this is the area of the database.

Recall that a database must include the field names of the columns of data as the first row of the database. If you wish to verify that the field names are included in the worksheet area H37..L158, type Q (QUIT). This step allows you to leave the Lotus 1-2-3 database query command menu. Now you can press the GoTo function key, F5, and type H37 at the Lotus 1-2-3 prompt. After verifying that the field names are included, press the Home key to return to cell A1.

If you reviewed the contents of row 37, you will have to reaccess the Lotus 1-2-3 database query commands with /DQ (DATA QUERY). To complete the "creation of the database," two other commands must be executed. First, an output range must be established; second, a criterion must be established. The purpose of establishing an output range is to provide a space on the worksheet for listing the cases that you extract from the database. The purpose of establishing a criterion is to give Lotus 1-2-3 a basis for extracting records from the data file.

With the Lotus 1-2-3 database query command menu at the top of the screen, type O (OUTPUT). Note that cells A10..C14 are highlighted because the range A10..C14 was previously entered at the following Lotus 1-2-3 prompt:

Enter Output range:

Notice that five rows are highlighted. The top row in the highlighted area contains the field names. In this case, there are three field names: Name, Race, and Sex. Any of the field names which are included in the input range of the database could have been duplicated here, but only these three were chosen. Lotus 1-2-3 will only output data for those fields that are included in the output range. Be sure to press the Enter key to retain the stored output area and to cause Lotus 1-2-3 to display the database query commands once again.

The final command necessary to establish the parameters of a data base is the criterion command. Type C (CRITERION). Notice that cells C7..D8 are highlighted. Press the Enter key to retain this area of the worksheet as the stored criterion. (Previously, the two fields named Race and Sex were typed into this section of the spreadsheet since it is on the basis of race and sex that we wish to select employee data.)

Notice that a B is typed below the field, Race, and a M is typed below the field, Sex. The B stands for Black, and the M stands for male. These same symbols are used in the database under the field names Race and Sex. Notice also that the code for Black (B) and the code for male (M) are in the same row. When two codes are in the same row as in this situation, Lotus 1-2-3 treats the codes as being connected by the word _and_. Thus, Lotus 1-2-3 will extract data based on the criterion of an employee's being Black _and_ male. If these codes had been in separate rows (for example, the B in row 8 and the M in row 9) with all three rows being part of the criterion, then Lotus 1-2-3 would have treated the two codes as having been connected with the word _or_. In this alternative situation, Lotus 1-2-3 would have extracted data based on the criterion of an employee's being Black _or_ male, resulting in a larger number of cases being extracted from the database. However, in order to count the number of Black males only, you want Lotus 1-2-3 to extract only those employees who are both Black _and_ male.

Since we included three of the fields from the database in the output area, data for these three fields will be extracted for Black male employees. To extract this information from the database, type E (Extract). Data for each Black male employee will be listed automatically in the output area of the worksheet. To return to the Ready mode of Lotus 1-2-3, type Q (QUIT).

Here it is obvious how many employees were extracted from the database. Sometimes this number will not be so obvious when there are a large number of employees. To use Lotus 1-2-3 to count for you when there are a larger number of cases to be counted, you should learn to use the Lotus 1-2-3 statistical function @COUNT. With Lotus 1-2-3 in the Ready mode (without a menu at the top of the screen), move the cursor to cell C15 and enter the statistical function @COUNT to count the number of cases that were extracted from the database. This statistical function takes the following form:

@COUNT (C11..C14)

Lotus 1-2-3 will then count the number of entries in the area of the worksheet specified by the argument C11..C14.

Building the Utilization Table. If you were to follow the procedure for the second portion of the output screen that you have just used to count employees by racial and sex category, you would have to change the codes below the field names Race and Sex in the criterion section of the spreadsheet for each category of employees. You would also have to provide separate output areas for each of the changes in the criterion. Then you would have to count the number of employees extracted and written in each output range.

A shorter method is available for completing this analysis and building a utilization table. This method will provide the same results as the one you just used, but it will avoid the need to actually list the data on the employees in each racial and sex category. After all, you are only interested in the count of employees in a category, and it would be convenient to have tabular results.

Move the cursor so that the area A16..G32 of the worksheet appears on the screen. Your task is to fill this table. A special database statistical function may be used to provide the required information (indicated by highlighted zeros) in columns B and C for each category of employees. This database statistical function has the following general format:

@DCOUNT (input,offset,criterion)

Notice that this command begins with the word @DCOUNT. Its name indicates that it is a counting function, but the word COUNT is preceded by the letter D, which stands for database. This function takes the place of the procedures that you just used to count Black males.

The database statistical function, @DCOUNT, has three arguments--the three parts within parentheses set off from one another by commas. The first and last arguments (input and criterion) of the database statistical function have the same meaning that they had in the Data Query command you used when working with the first portion of the output screen. That is, the Input is the area of a database, including its field names at the top of the columns; the Criterion is the area of the worksheet in which the selected field names with their accompanying codes are located. The middle argument, Offset, is new. It is always an integer, and it specifies how many columns removed from the left-most column of the input range the function is to operate on.

Cell C24 contains the following example of a database statistical function:

@DCOUNT (H37..L158,0,C7..D8)

This database statistical function counts the number of Black males. The input range (H37..L158) is the same as the range that you used when working with the first portion of the output screen. The criterion range (C7..D8) is also the same as the criterion range that you used when working with the first portion of the output screen. The offset is zero (0).

Thus, the operation (i.e., counting) called for by this database statistical function will be done on the first column of the area identified as the input. Since Lotus 1-2-3 is just counting the number of employees selected based on the criterion, it does not matter which of the columns of the input area you ask Lotus 1-2-3 to work on.

Complete the remainder of the utilization table by entering database statistical functions for each zero (0) in cells B22..C30. You will need a separate criterion for each entry; these criteria are located in cells A40..C57.

Begin by counting the number of Asian females. Move the cursor to cell B22. Type the following in cell B22:

@DCOUNT(H37..L158,0,

This portion of the function @DCOUNT establishes the input area as the slice of the database in this Lotus 1-2-3 file, and it indicates to Lotus 1-2-3 that operations should be completed on the first column of the database. After typing this portion of the entry (and before pressing the Enter key), move the cursor to B40. Notice that cell A40 indicates that this is the criterion for Asian females. Below the field names for Race and Sex are the codes A for Asian and F for Female. Now type a period and move the cursor to C41. Notice that the criterion area of B40..C41 is highlighted. Type a right parenthesis. This will cause Lotus 1-2-3 to return the cursor to cell B22. Enter the function in cell B22. The database statistical function that you will see at the upper left of the screen is:

@DCOUNT(H37..L158,0,B40..C41)

and the number entered in cell B22 is zero. There are no Asian females in this slice of the HR Database of Metro Hospital. Following the procedure just described, enter database statistical functions for each of the zeros in cells B22..C30.

Utilization analyses usually contain the percentage of an organization's employees that each racial and sex group represents. To calculate these percentages, you must add the entries for each sex and racial group. The function @SUM is useful for accomplishing this. For example, move the cursor to cell D22 and type @SUM(. Before entering the function, move the cursor to cell B22, type a period, move the cursor to cell C22, and type a right parenthesis. Lotus 1-2-3 will move the cursor back to cell D22. You may now press the Enter key.

In column D of the utilization table are five more zeros (cells D24, D26, D28, D30, and D32). Copy the statistical function @SUM from cell D22 to each of these cells in turn by moving the cursor to cell D24. Access the Lotus 1-2-3 main menu and the Copy command by typing /C (COPY). At the following Lotus 1-2-3 prompt:

Enter range to copy FROM:D24..D24

press the Escape key and move the cursor to cell D22. This is the cell from which you wish to copy the statistical function @SUM. Then press the Enter key. Lotus 1-2-3 will record cell D22 as the cell from which you wish to copy, and it will return the cursor to cell D24, the cell to which you wish to copy some information. At the following Lotus 1-2-3 prompt, press the Enter key:

Enter range to copy TO:D24

The statistical function @SUM contained in cell D22 will be copied to cell D24, but it will be modified in the manner described in the section on The Copy Command in Chapter 2.

Cells B32 and C32 require the totals for all females and males. Simply enter the statistical function @SUM in cell B32 to add the entries in cells B22..B30. Then copy this function to cell C32.

The reader of this utilization table can better understand the relative number of employees in each category by calculating the percentage of the total number of employees represented by each category. Notice that cell D32 contains a grand total for all employees in all categories. It is the sum of males and females. Use this sum as the denominator in your calculations of percentages in the cells containing zeros in the worksheet area E22..F30. For example, enter the following formula in cell E22:

+B22/$D$32

This formula looks somewhat similar to the ones you read about in Chapter 2; however, it contains dollar signs on both sides of the column labeled D. These dollar signs tell Lotus 1-2-3 that cell D32 is an absolute value in this formula. When copied to another cell, it remains exactly as it is. This is a convenient feature of Lotus 1-2-3 since it allows you to copy this formula to the remaining cells in columns E and F for which there is a highlighted zero (0) in the utilization table. When copying the formula, the numerator will change; but the denominator--the grand total number of employees--will remain the same. Now copy the formula in cell E22 to the remaining cells in columns E and F for which there is a highlighted zero.

Your final task in completing the utilization table is to use the statistical function @SUM to find the total percentage of each racial group in column G of the table. Once you have entered the appropriate statistical function @SUM in cell G22, you may copy it to cells G24, G26, G28, and G30. The statistical function @SUM is already entered in cells E32..G32. These cells provide percentages for females, males, and the whole group, respectively. Cell G32 should be 100%; it is a check on your earlier calculations.

Saving Your Worksheets

Type /FS (FILE SAVE) to access the Lotus 1-2-3 file command menu and the specific save command of this menu. Lotus 1-2-3 will respond with the name of the file on which you are working, EEO1. Press the Enter key in order to indicate that this filename is the one under which you wish to save the current worksheet. Since you replaced the HR Data Diskette with your Working Diskette, Lotus 1-2-3 will proceed to save this file under the name EEO1 on the Working Diskette. If you subsequently retrieve EEO1 from the Working Diskette and then save it, Lotus 1-2-3 will respond with:

Cancel   Replace

Type R (REPLACE) and Lotus 1-2-3 will write the changes you have made over the old file on the Working Diskette.

Printing the Results

Return to cell A1. Type /PP (PRINT PRINTER) to access the Lotus 1-2-3 print menu of commands. With the menu at the top of the screen, type R (RANGE). Notice that the print range of A1..G32 is highlighted, and this range is entered at the top of the screen:

Enter print range: A1..G32

Press the Enter key to confirm that this range is the area of the worksheet you want to print. Check to see that your printer is ready and the paper is aligned correctly with the top of the page of paper as the first line to be printed. Now type AG (ALIGN GO). These commands will cause Lotus 1-2-3 to treat the current page position in your printer as the top of the page, and printing will begin.

After the printer stops, type P (PAGE) to advance to the top of the next page of paper in your printer. Type Q (QUIT) to leave the Lotus 1-2-3 print command menu.

Analyzing the Results

You are now ready to use the information that you have obtained from the HR Database to complete an EEO-1 form and evaluate your selection and retention decisions. In the space provided, answer the questions at the end of this chapter. Then tear out that page, attach it to the printed results, and turn both in to your instructor.

Questions

1. How does this organization's being a hospital explain the distribution of employees?

2. What information do you need to evaluate the appropriateness of the distribution of employees by sex and racial category?

3. What recommendations would you make to the HR staff to follow up these analyses?

CHAPTER 5
EQUAL EMPLOYMENT OPPORTUNITY AND AFFIRMATIVE ACTION: UNDERUTILIZATION ANALYSIS

Lotus 1-2-3 applications in this chapter:

Command Menus
   FILE
   PRINT
   COPY
Mathematical Operations
   Subtraction
   Multiplication
Statistical Functions
   @SUM
Database Statistical Functions
   @DCOUNT

Chapter Outline

Background of the Exercise
Retrieving EEO2
Output Screen
Input Screen
Analysis
   Building the Utilization Table
   Building the Underutilization Table
Saving Your Worksheets
Printing the Results
Analyzing the Results

Underutilization refers to the failure of an organization to hire persons in particular job categories, such as nursing, in the same proportion that they are available in the labor area from which persons may be recruited. Underutilization analysis is critical to the development of an affirmative action plan. As a result of the analysis, a company determines whether it has employed insufficient numbers of persons from protected classes (racial minorities, handicapped persons, and women). After reaching a conclusion that there is underutilization, an employer can establish hiring or promotion goals in order to correct the underutilization and achieve **parity** (percentage of persons in an affected class within the organization approximately equal to the percentage availability in the labor pool).

Background of the Exercise

To evaluate whether underutilization exists, two elements are required. First, the organization must determine the utilization rate for a given job category. This requirement is relatively straightforward if one possesses a HR database that contains information about race, sex, and job category. The requirement may be satisfied by following the procedures outlined in Chapter 4 for a given job category.

The second requirement for evaluating underutilization is possessing information about the availability within the labor pool of women and other members of affected classes within a given job category. Obtaining this information is complicated by a number of factors. For example, there may be variations in the use of a job title within the labor market. Thus, all persons listed as medical technicians may not possess the same skills and experience. Even if it can be determined that the persons listed as medical technicians are in fact medical technicians from the point of view of a given recruiter, there still may be variations in the skill level, such that all are not capable of filling the need. Furthermore, it must be determined that the available persons are in a geographical area that makes them recruitable by a given employer. This final issue is a judgment about the appropriateness of the geographical area for the labor market.

Practically speaking, an underutilization analysis may result in a hospital's obtaining information from the labor market which indicates that 51 percent of physical therapists are female. If the percentage of females at the hospital is below 51, then underutilization is demonstrated. Therefore, affirmative action goals may be set in order to hire sufficient numbers of female physical therapists, thereby eliminating the underutilization and achieving parity. Achieving parity means hiring enough female physical therapists so that the percentage within the hospital (e.g., 51%) will be at least equal to the 51 percent of available female therapists.

This chapter provides you an opportunity to complete an underutilization analysis for the job category of Staff Nurse as the foundation for the establishment of hiring goals. Your task is (1) to determine if there is underutilization in the affected classes for this job category, and (2) to develop hiring goals, where appropriate, for women and minorities within the Staff Nurse job category. To accomplish these two tasks, you must complete a utilization table and an underutilization table for the job category of Staff Nurse.

Retrieving EEO2

Retrieve the file **EEO2** from your copy of the HR Data Diskette. (If you are having difficulty, you may wish to review the sections on Getting Started and Lotus 1-2-3 Command Menus in Chapter 2, or you may wish to obtain the help of the computer laboratory assistant or your instructor.) After retrieving EEO2, remember to remove the HR Data Diskette from your computer's drive. In its place, insert the Working Diskette that you are using to save files, such as EEO2, after you have completed your analyses.

Output Screen

The output screen is located in cells A1..N21 (see Exhibit 5-1). The first portion of the output screen is the utilization table in cells A1..G21. The second portion of the output screen is the underutilization table in cells I5..N21.

The first portion of the output screen is very similar to the utilization table you completed in Chapter 4, However, in this chapter the utilization table is for only one job category--Staff Nurse. The second portion of the output screen incorporates data from the utilization table along with information about availability in the labor market.

Input Screen

This slice of the database is the same as the one you worked with in Chapter 4. It contains fields for the employee's name, race, sex, job title, and department. It is located in cells O24..S146.

Analysis

Building the Utilization Table. Your first task is to build the utilization table by using the statistical database function @DCOUNT for counting the number of persons in each racial and sex category. Therefore, return to cell A1 if the cursor is not already there. Columns B and C of the utilization table contain highlighted zeros to indicate that you must supply something in order to complete the table. The general form of the database statistical function is:

@DCOUNT(input,offset,criterion)

This is the database statistical function that you saw in Chapter 4. Its name indicates that it is a counting function, but the word COUNT is preceded by the letter D, which stands for Database. This database statistical function takes the place of using the Data Query commands of Lotus 1-2-3 to extract data and then count the records.

The first argument, Input, in the database statistical function refers to the area of the database, including the field names above each column of data. The second argument is Offset, and it specifies how many columns removed from the left-most column of the input range Lotus 1-2-3 is to operate on. The third argument, Criterion, refers to the area of the worksheet in which the selected field names with their accompanying codes are located. (If you need more information about this database statistical function, review the section on Output Screen 2 in Chapter 4.)

Exhibit 5-1

EEO2
EEO and Affirmative Action: Underutilization Analysis
Name:

OUTPUT SCREEN

UTILIZATION TABLE

RACE	SEX			PERCENTAGES		
	FEMALE	MALE	SUM	FEMALE	MALE	TOTAL
ASIAN	0	0	0	0.0%	0.0%	0.0%
BLACK	0	0	0	0.0%	0.0%	0.0%
NATIVE AMERICAN	0	0	0	0.0%	0.0%	0.0%
WHITE, HISPANIC ORIGIN	0	0	0	0.0%	0.0%	0.0%
WHITE, NON HISPANIC	0	0	0	0.0%	0.0%	0.0%
TOTALS	0	0	0	0.0%	0.0%	0.0%

UNDERUTILIZATION TABLE

	AVAILABILITY		TARGET		UNDERUTILIZED	
	FEMALE	MALE	FEMALE	MALE	FEMALE	MALE
ASIAN	6.1%	0.1%	0.0	0.0	0	0
BLACK	11.9%	0.3%	0.0	0.0	0	0
NATIVE AMERICAN	0.9%	0.1%	0.0	0.0	0	0
WHITE, HISPANIC ORIGIN	22.8%	0.2%	0.0	0.0	0	0
WHITE, NON HISPANIC	57.0%	0.6%	0.0	0.0	0	0
TOTALS	98.7%	1.3%				

As an aid to completing the utilization table, the following statistical formula is located in cell B11:

$$@DCOUNT(O25..S146,0,B28..D29)$$

This function includes the input argument (O25..S146)--the entire database with its field names and the data below each field name.

As before, the offset is zero since this function may count any column of the database that meets the specifications of the criterion. The criterion (A27..D47) differs from the criterion in Chapter 4 in that it includes the job title as well as the racial and sex groups. Thus, records which are counted by this database statistical function must match the specified job (Staff Nurse), the specified racial group, and the specified sex group.

You may wish to review the section of the worksheet which contains the various criteria that are necessary to complete the utilization table. The criteria are located in cells A27..D47. Press the GoTo function key, F5. Then enter A27 at the Lotus 1-2-3 prompt. Below the word CRITERION you will notice the field names and the appropriate codes that have already been established for each of the race, sex, and job title categories contained in the utilization table. Notice that each criterion differs from those in Chapter 4 in that the field name, Job Title, and the particular job in which you are interested, Staff Nurse, is included as a part of each criterion.

Return to cell A5 and use the database statistical function @DCOUNT to calculate the count for each ethnic and gender category of employees: Asian females and males, Black females and males, Native American females and males, White Hispanic origin females and males, and White non-Hispanic females and males. Since the @DCOUNT database statistical function is already entered in cell B11, you may begin with cell C11, the count of Asian males.

The database statistical function that you will enter in cell C11 is very similar to the model in cell B11. Notice that the entry in cell B11 looks like this:

$$@DCOUNT(O25..S146,0,B28..D29)$$

The form that you will use in cell C11 will have only one change--the location of the criterion (B28..D29). The input area of the database (O25..S146) will remain the same, and the offset (the zero) will remain the same. The offset is zero since it does not matter which column of the database Lotus 1-2-3 counts.

Review the section of the worksheet in which the criteria are located (A27..D47). There you will see that the criterion for Asian males is located at B30..D31. Thus, the correct format of the @DCOUNT database statistical function for cell C11 is:

@DCOUNT(O25..S146,0,B30..D31)

You should now enter the correct forms of the @DCOUNT database statistical functions for the females and males of the following ethnic or racial groups: Blacks, Native Americans, Whites of Hispanic origin, and Whites of non-Hispanic origin. These @DCOUNT database statistical functions should be entered in cells B13, B15, B17, B19, C13, C15, C17, and C19.

Column D of the output screen requests a sum, or total number, of persons from each ethnic or racial group. Enter the appropriate form of the @SUM statistical function in cell D11:

@SUM(B11..C11)

You may copy this statistical function to the following cells in column D: D13, D15, D17, and D19. (You may obtain help in using the Copy command from Chapter 2 or the example in Chapter 4.) Since there are blank rows in column D of the output screen (e.g., D14, D16), you will have to copy the @SUM statistical function one cell at a time.

After having copied the @SUM statistical functions for each ethnic and gender group, use the @SUM statistical function to find the totals in cells B21, C21, and D21. Begin by finding the total number of females in column B. Then copy this formula to cells C21 and D21.

The reader of this utilization table can better understand the relative number of employees in each racial or ethnic category by calculating the percentage of the total number of staff nurses represented by each category (columns E, F, and G). Notice that cell D21 contains a grand total for male and female staff nurses. Use this cell as the denominator in calculating the percentages of staff nurses represented by each ethnic and gender group. For example, enter the following formula in cell E11:

+B11/$D$21

This formula looks similar to the ones you read about in Chapter 2. However, it contains dollar signs on both sides of the column D label. These dollar signs tell Lotus 1-2-3 that cell D21 is an absolute value in this formula. When copied to another cell, D21 will not change. This is a convenient feature of Lotus 1-2-3 because it allows you to copy this formula to the remaining cells in columns E, F, and G for which there are highlighted zeros in the utilization table. When copying the formula, the numerator will change; but the denominator--the grand total of staff nurses--will remain the same. Now copy the formula in cell E11 to cells F11, G11, E13, F13, G13, E15, F15, G15, E17, F17, G17, E19, F19, and G19. After completing this copying, notice that the percentage in cell G21 should equal 100%.

Building the Underutilization Table. Use the GoTo function key, F5, to move the cursor over to I6. In columns I and J of the underutilization table are the availability percentages for the Staff Nurse job from Metro Hospital's labor area. Notice that more than 98 percent of available nurses are women (see cell I21), and less than 2 percent are men (see cell J21).

In columns K and L, calculate the targets that Metro Hospital should meet to reach parity in each racial and sex category. A target assumes that Metro Hospital should have a representative number of staff nurses from each ethnic and gender group. That would be parity. For example, if 25 percent of the available nurses in the labor market area were females of Hispanic origin and a hospital had 100 staff nurses, the target would be 25 (i.e., .25*100).

Targets may be calculated from two pieces of information: (1) the actual count of staff nurses in the racial and sex category from the utilization table, and (2) the availability percentage in the labor market area from the underutilization table. For example, the target for females of Asian origin is calculated by multiplying the labor market area availability percentage (6.1%) in cell I11 by the total number of staff nurses in cell D21, as follows:

$$+I11*\$D\$21$$

In this formula, the cell address for the total number of staff nurses is written as an absolute cell address to indicate that the cell address is not variable. (You do not want Lotus 1-2-3 to vary this cell address as you copy the formula to the remaining cells with highlighted zeros in columns K and L.) Go ahead and copy the formula from K11 to the remaining cells with highlighted zeros in columns K and L.

You are now ready to calculate the underutilization for each ethnic and gender category by subtracting the actual count of staff nurses in each category from the target number. Thus, enter the following formula in cell M11:

$$+K11-B11$$

This formula subtracts the actual number of Asian females from the targeted number of Asian females. Remember that the targeted number is what Metro would have with an exact distribution of its staff nurses over the ethnic and gender groups as they are represented in the labor market area.

Copy this formula to the remaining cells with highlighted zeroes in columns M and N. Notice that this formula will result in a positive number if the target is larger than the actual number of employees. In other words, there will be a positive number if there is underutilization.

Saving Your Worksheets

Type /FS (FILE SAVE) to access the Lotus 1-2-3 command menu and the specific save command of this menu. Lotus 1-2-3 will respond with the name of the file on which you are working, EEO2. Press the Enter key to indicate that this filename is the one under which you wish to save the current worksheet. Since you replaced the HR Data Diskette with your Working Diskette, Lotus 1-2-3 will proceed to save this file under the name EEO2 on the Working Diskette. If you subsequently retrieve EEO2 from the Working Diskette and then save it, Lotus 1-2-3 will respond with:

Cancel   Replace

Then type R (REPLACE). Lotus 1-2-3 will write the changes you have made over the old file on the Working Diskette.

Printing the Results

Return to cell A1. Type /PP (PRINT PRINTER) to access the Lotus 1-2-3 print menu of commands. Print the two tables separately.

Begin with the utilization table. Type R (RANGE), and Lotus 1-2-3 will prompt you with:

Enter Print range:A1

Type a period and move the cursor to G21. The area of A5..G21 will be highlighted. By pressing the Enter key, you will store this area of the worksheet as the print range.

Check to see that the printer is ready and the paper is aligned correctly with the top of the page of paper as the first line to be printed. Now type AG (ALIGN GO). After the printer stops, type L (LINE) two or three times in order to provide some space between the utilization table and the underutilization table.

Now print the underutilization table. With the Lotus 1-2-3 print command menu still at the top of the screen, type CR (CLEAR RANGE). This command will erase the range that you stored to print the utilization table. Type R (RANGE). When Lotus 1-2-3 responds with the following prompt:

Enter Print Range:

respond with I6..N21. This range includes the area of the underutilization table. Press the Enter key to store the range.

To identify the racial groups, you should create a border column. Type OBC (OPTIONS BORDERS COLUMNS). At the following Lotus 1-2-3 prompt:

Enter Border Columns:

type A6 and press the Enter key. Now press Q (QUIT) to return to the main Print menu. Proceed to print Output Screen 2 just as you printed Output Screen 1. Type Q (QUIT) to leave the Lotus 1-2-3 print command menu.

Analyzing the Results

You are now ready to evaluate the degree to which Metro Hospital is underutilized in the job category of Staff Nurse. In the space provided, answer the questions at the end of this chapter. Then tear out that page, attach it to the printed results, and turn both in to your instructor.

Questions

1. In what racial and ethnic groups are you most likely to find job applicants for the position of Staff Nurse? (Hint: Look at the availability section of the underutilization table.)

2. In what areas should you set affirmative action goals? What goals should you set? (Hint: Positive numbers indicate underutilization in columns M and N of the underutilization table.)

3. What actions can you take to alter the available pool of Staff Nurse applicants?

CHAPTER 6
SELECTION: THE APPLICANT-TRACKING SYSTEM

Lotus 1-2-3 applications in this chapter:

Command Menus
  FILE
  PRINT
  COPY
  DATA QUERY

Chapter Outline

The selection process is a critical part of the management of an organization. Traditional views of management describe the functions of a manager as planning, organizing, directing, controlling, and staffing. More recent views describe a manager's functions in terms of selecting, leading, and motivating employees. Whether management is viewed from the more traditional functions or the more recent ones, selection is clearly recognized as a fundamental function of management. In fact, selection may be the function with which we can most improve organizational productivity.

Selection is a decision-making activity, and the quality of the decision making can be improved. It can be broken down into its subparts. For example, the application form--one of the typical parts of the selection process--can be structured to collect information which is known to be critical to job performance. The application form and all other subparts of the selection process may be examined for their validity, i.e., their ability to predict later performance of the employee. Where certain parts of the selection process possess low validity, alterations may be made to enhance their validity. Thus, the selection process offers managers the opportunity to review and manipulate the process with the goal of improving employee performance.

If an organization is to be successful in its evaluation of the selection process, it must retain records of the evaluations of applicants, including the results of tests given to applicants. An **applicant-tracking system** is a subpart of many HR databases. It permits one to record information about an applicant and analyze that data later. Typically an applicant-tracking system contains information about an applicant's having completed various stages in the application process. It may contain scores on tests that are a part of the application process, and it may contain ratings from such aspects of the process as the employment interview. Such information allows the staff of a HR department to (1) follow what is happening to an applicant as he or she is processed and evaluated, and (2) analyze the evaluations of applicants in light of the ultimate decision to offer or not offer a position.

Background of the Exercise

Metro Hospital has employed a part of its HR Database as an applicant-tracking system. Thus, its staff members have been able to determine when to call applicants in for testing or for a physical examination. Unfortunately, Metro has made little use of the system for analyzing its selection system and the evaluation process. Therefore, the Metro Hospital HR Department staff has decided to review the tracking system for one of its largest job categories: staff nurses.

Metro's HR staff is concerned only with people who made applications since 1980. The staff is interested in examining the differences between applicants to whom it has offered positions and those to whom it has declined to offer positions. The staff is also interested in those applicants to whom it has made offers but who have declined the offers. From these analyses, the staff anticipates that it may want to formulate new policy.

Retrieving APPLCNT

To assist the staff in its analyses of applicants and the selection process, retrieve the Lotus 1-2-3 file called APPLCNT from your Human Resources Data Diskette. (Should you need some assistance, review the section on "Getting Started" in Chapter 2. You may also wish to obtain help from the computer laboratory assistant or your instructor.) After retrieving APPLCNT, remember to replace the HR Data Diskette with your Working Diskette on which you have been saving files after having completed your analyses.

Output Screen

The output area of your worksheet is A1..M72 (see Exhibits 6-1a and 6-1b). It includes three portions for which you must extract applicant records from this slice of the HR Database Applicant-Tracking System. The first portion is located in A8..M31. Here you are to extract the records of applicants to whom job offers have been made over the period under review.

Exhibit 6-1a

APPLCNT
Selection: The Applicant Tracking System
Name:

OUTPUT SCREEN

JOBS OFFERED
Criterion

JOB
OFFER

NAME	JOB TITLE	RECRUITMENT SOURCE	APPLICATION FORM	CERTIFICATE	SCREENING	INTERVIEW SUPERVISOR	INTERVIEW REFERENCES	CHECKED OFFER	JOB OFFER ACCEPTED	OFFER DATE OF HIRE	RACE	SEX

Exhibit 6-1b

JOB NOT OFFERED
Criterion

JOB
OFFER

NAME	JOB TITLE	RECRUITMENT SOURCE	APPLICATION FORM	CERTIFICATE	INTERVIEW SCREENING	INTERVIEW SUPERVISOR	CHECKED REFERENCES	JOB OFFER	OFFER ACCEPTED	DATE OF HIRE	RACE	SEX

FILE INCOMPLETE
Criterion

The second portion of the output screen is located in A35..M54. This area provides space for extracting and listing the applicant records for those applicants who were not offered a position as a result of the decisions made in the selection process.

The third portion of the output screen is provided for listing records of applicants who are still under consideration for a position or whose records show that the selection process is not complete. This area covers cells A58..M72.

Input Screen

This slice of the HR Database Applicant-Tracking System is located in A73..M104 and includes only data on staff nurses who have applied for a position with Metro Hospital since the early eighties. It contains the following fields for each applicant: Name, Job Title, Recruitment Source, Application Form (whether or not the application form has been completed), Certificate (whether or not the applicant possesses a certificate), Interview Screening (scores on the interview), Interview Supervisor (scores on this interview), Checked References (an indication of their having been checked), Job Offer, Offer Accepted, and Date of Hire.

Recruitment sources include universities, a private employment agency for which the hospital must pay a fee, unsolicited or "walk-in" applicants, recommendations of other employees, and recommendations from the union. An indication that an application form has been completed is recorded by a "Y" for Yes. Data about certification is recorded as "none" for no certificate, "temporary" for a temporary certificate, and "registered" for a staff nurse who holds a certification as a registered nurse.

Ratings on the Interview Screening are completed by trained interviewers in the HR Department. These interviewers rate interviewees on several subscales and the overall, global scale for which data are recorded in the applicant-tracking system. Ratings are high, medium, and low, indicating the interviewer's evaluation of the applicant's qualifications.

A similar global rating scale is also a part of the supervisor's interview ratings, and its results are recorded as a part of the applicant-tracking system. A "N" for No and a "Y" for Yes record whether references have been checked. A "N" for No and a "Y" for Yes record the decision to make a job offer and to record an applicant's decision to take the offer of a job. A "NA" in the field Offer Accepted indicates that this field is inapplicable since no offer was made. An "X" in any field indicates that the application process is not complete for an applicant whose application form has been received.

Although these data are the key parts of the hospital's applicant-tracking system, other data fields may be combined with the data from the tracking system for purposes of analysis. In the case of this analysis, three fields from the larger employee database were included: Hire Date, Race, and Sex. Normally these fields are not accessible to on-line users of the HR Database. Information about race and sex are recorded separately from the tracking system to avoid the introduction of bias into decisions. Thus, you will observe that there is no information about these three fields for applicants whose applications are still being processed.

Analysis

Applicants To Whom Jobs Have Been Offered. Your first step is to extract data about those applicants to whom jobs have been offered. Cells A9..A13 provide an area for the criterion on which this database search will be based. Since you want to extract those persons to whom jobs have been offered, enter the alphanumeric character "Y" for "Yes" as the criterion. This data entry should be made in cell A13, and it should be entered as an upper case "Y" since the criterion and input range information must exactly match.

Access the Lotus 1-2-3 database query menu of commands to "create a database." (If you need help in accessing this set of Lotus 1-2-3 commands, review the section on the Database Query command in Chapter 2.) The first step is to define the input area of the worksheet. With the Lotus 1-2-3 database query commands at the top of the screen, type I (INPUT). At the following Lotus 1-2-3 prompt:

Enter Input range:

enter the coordinates of the cells which bound the slice of the database contained in this file. To do this, move the cursor to the first field name in the upper left corner of the database: this is cell A75. As usual, type a period to establish the range; then move the cursor to the lower right cell of the database. Pressing the Enter key will complete the steps in defining the database and return you to the Lotus 1-2-3 database query command menu.

Your next step is to define the criterion. Type C (CRITERION) and move the cursor to A12. Type a period and move the cursor to A13 to include the value you had earlier entered in cell A13. Pressing the Enter key will store the criterion with its label and value and return you to the Data Query menu.

Although the name of this field includes two rows with the words JOB OFFER, only the word OFFER is included in the stored criterion area. You may recall from the description of database query commands in Chapter 2 that only the field name which is immediately adjacent and above the data is considered by Lotus 1-2-3 to be the field name. The other label, JOB, is useful to the reader in understanding the field, but it is unnecessary to Lotus 1-2-3 in carrying out its operations.

The last step in creating the database is to define an area of the worksheet into which Lotus 1-2-3 can write the results of its database in-

70

quiry (i.e., the extracted cases). This is the area into which the information about each applicant to whom a job offer was made will be written by Lotus 1-2-3. Type O (OUTPUT) and move the cursor to A16. Type a period and move the cursor to cell M31. Pressing the Enter key will store the output area. Notice that you included space for writing the extracted cases, and you included the field names for the various fields from the database for which you want Lotus 1-2-3 to write information.

The final step in this part of the analysis is to extract the records that match the criterion, i.e., those records that contain a "Y" for Yes in the field Offer. Type E (Extract) to extract these records. Then return to the Ready mode of Lotus 1-2-3 by typing Q (QUIT).

Applicants to Whom No Jobs Have Been Offered. Move the cursor to A35. This second portion of the output screen is designed to extract information about those applicants to whom no job offer was made. Follow procedures similar to those used in extracting information about the applicants to whom job offers were made. The distinction lies in the criterion. At cell A40, enter the code "N" for No. Remember to use an upper case "N" since the criterion must exactly match the data within the input range. Now continue with the procedures that you followed for the first portion of the output screen.

Begin by accessing the Lotus 1-2-3 command menu for database inquiries: /DQ (Data Query). Before defining the Input, Criterion, and Output areas, type R (Reset) to erase the previous definitions of each of these commands. Remember to include the field names as the first row in the input area. Your output area should be defined as A43..M54. The criterion area is A39..A40. After extracting the cases that match this criterion, quit the database query command menu and return to the Ready mode of Lotus 1-2-3.

Applicants on Whom No Decision on a Job Offer Has Been Made. The final part of the analysis is to extract the records of those applicants who are still in the application process and for whom no decision on an offer has been made. Having quit the database query command menu of Lotus 1-2-3, you should be in the Ready mode. Move the cursor to A58. Notice that this third portion of the output screen differs from the first and second portions. Whereas the first two portions contained the field name for the criterion and the field names below which extracted cases were written, this third portion is blank.

Thus, your first step is to type the field name for the criterion, the appropriate code for those who have incomplete files, and the field names from the database for which you want Lotus 1-2-3 to write information about the extracted cases. (To complete these tasks, you may wish to review the criterion for the second portion of the output screen and the field names from the database.)

Begin this first step of the final part of the analysis by entering in cells A61..A63 the complete name (both rows) of the criterion and the

71

code for those who have incomplete files. (If you do not recall the code for those whose files are incomplete, review Exhibit 6-2 of this chapter.) Then enter the required field names from the database in rows 65 and 66, beginning with A65. (An easy way to do this is to use the Lotus 1-2-3 Copy command to copy the field names from the database. Chapter 2 provides assistance in using this Lotus 1-2-3 command.)

In establishing the output range for the extracted cases, use the area A66..M69. You are now ready to extract the records of those applicants who are still in the application process and for whom no decision on an offer has been made.

Saving Your Worksheets

Type /FS (FILE SAVE) to access the Lotus 1-2-3 file command menu. Save the file onto the Working Diskette rather than the HR Data Diskette. (If you want to assure yourself that you are using the correct Lotus 1-2-3 commands, review the section on Retrieving and Saving Files in Chapter 2.)

Printing the Results

Before beginning to print the results, check to see that you have edited cell A3 and typed your name after the word **Name:**. Since the results cover more than the width of the screen, you will need to print the results in two steps.

Begin by moving the cursor to cell A1. Type /PP (PRINT PRINTER) to access the Lotus 1-2-3 print command menu. Select the range by typing (Range) and a period. Then move the cursor to E69. Press the Enter key to store this range. Now make sure that your printer is ready and the paper is properly aligned. Type AG (ALIGN GO).

After printing this section of the results, the main Print command will return to the top of the screen. You may now clear the stored range for the previous section of output by typing CR (CLEAR RANGE). Establish the range for the remainder of the output screen by typing R (RANGE). When Lotus 1-2-3 responds with the following prompt:

Enter Print range:

type F8..M69 and press the Enter key. To interpret this part of the output screen that you are printing, it is helpful to have the A column as well as the F to M columns printed. You can do this by typing OBC (OPTIONS BORDERS COLUMNS). At the following Lotus 1-2-3 prompt:

Enter Border Columns:

type A1 for the far-left column of the worksheet. After pressing the Enter key, type Q (QUIT) to leave the Options submenu and return to the main print command menu. Type P (PAGE) to move the printer to the top of the page. Proceed to print these results. Type G (GO) to print the remainder of the output screen. Quit the print command menu by typing Q (QUIT).

Analyzing the Results

You may now evaluate the Applicant-Tracking System and the decisions that have resulted during the selection process. To do this, in the space provided answer the questions at the end of this chapter. Then tear out that page, attach it to the printed results, and turn both in to your instructor.

Questions

1. Which recruitment sources seem to be responsible for the largest number of applicants? Would you recommend targeting any of these sources for additional recruitment?

2. What aspects of the application process seem to be most highly associated with making a job offer?

3. In what ways may you use these data to improve your recruiting of members of protected classes?

4. How would you use the information about those persons whose files are
   incomplete?

CHAPTER 7
SELECTION: ADVERSE IMPACT

Lotus 1-2-3 applications in this chapter:

Command Menus
    FILE
    PRINT
    COPY
Mathematical Operations
    Multiplication
    Division*
Statistical Functions
    @MAX*
Logical Functions
    @IF*

Chapter Outline

Background of the Exercise
Retrieving ADVERSE
Output Screen
Analysis
    Determining the Percentage Selected of the Number Who Applied
    Determining the Existence or Nonexistence of Adverse Impact
Saving Your Worksheets
Printing the Results
Analyzing the Results

Adverse impact refers to a significantly greater rejection rate of a member of a protected class (e.g., Hispanics) for selection, promotion, or retention when compared with the group for which there is the highest rate of selection, promotion, or retention.[1]

Adverse impact may be calculated in a variety of ways. One way is provided by the Uniform Guidelines[2] which defines **adverse impact** in the selection process as a selection rate (for protected groups) which is less than four-fifths (80 percent) of the rate of the group with the highest selection rate. Adverse impact may also be demonstrated by showing that there is a statistically significant lower selection rate for members of a protected group when compared with the selection rate for members of a nonprotected group such as White males.

_____
    *Indicates a first-time use of this Lotus 1-2-3 application in this book.

Unfortunately, many companies find themselves in the difficult position of analyzing information about their selection patterns and discovering adverse impact only after someone has filed a complaint with the state or federal Office of Equal Employment Opportunity. As a result of the complaint, an organization is forced to examine the impact of its selection, retention, or promotion decisions on members of protected classes.

One of the past reasons for this tardy analysis may have been the inaccessibility of information about selection or the absence of easily used computer information systems. With the advent of easy-to-use HR information systems and readily available and inexpensive computer systems, there is little reason for an organization to fail to analyze its selection patterns.

Background of the Exercise

Metro Hospital maintains extensive information about its job applicants. In addition to allowing its HR staff to manage easily the recruitment and selection process, the information may also be used to determine whether there is adverse impact in the selection process. By analyzing the data for adverse impact, Metro Hospital is able to correct a problem, if it exists, before it leads to official complaints or legal battles. Furthermore, such analysis puts the hospital in a good position to defend itself, should there be an unwarranted complaint concerning discrimination.

To evaluate its own policy of nondiscrimination in employment decision making, the HR Department at Metro Hospital has decided to determine if there is any overall adverse impact in its selection process. Although the staff may use a test of statistical significance for determining adverse impact, the small number of applicants suggests that the 80:20 rule (sometimes known as the four-fifths rule) from the Uniform Guidelines is preferable. Initially the staff decided to analyze adverse impact within the job category of Laboratory Technician.

Retrieving ADVERSE

To complete the analysis for the staff, retrieve the file called ADVERSE from your HR Data Diskette. (Should you need some assistance, review the section on Getting Started in Chapter 2. You may also wish to obtain help from the computer laboratory assistant or your instructor.) After retrieving ADVERSE from your HR Data Diskette, remember to replace the HR Data Diskette with your Working Diskette on which you have been saving files after completing your analyses.

Output Screen

The output screen is the only screen in this file. It covers cells A1..F24 (see Exhibit 7-1).

Exhibit 7-1

ADVERSE
Selection: Adverse Impact
Name:

OUPUT SCREEN
Laboratory Technician

Sex/Race	Number Selected	Number Applied	Percentage Selected	80% of Base Rate	Adverse Impact
FEMALES					
Asian	0	2	0%	0%	0
Black	2	6	0%	0%	0
Hispanic	2	5	0%	0%	0
Native	1	2	0%	0%	0
White	6	15	0%	0%	0
MALES					
Asian	0	2	0%	0%	0
Black	1	4	0%	0%	0
Hispanic	3	5	0%	0%	0
Native	0	1	0%	0%	0
White	5	8	0%	0%	0

Data were already extracted from the HR Database for the following groups of females and males concerning the number of persons selected and the number of persons who applied: Asian, Black, Hispanic, Native American, and White non-Hispanic. Column A, beginning at cell A11, lists the protected racial and ethnic groups separately for females and males.

Other fields in the output screen are: Number Selected, Number Applied, Percentage Selected, 80% of Base Rate, and Adverse Impact. Column B (Number Selected) contains the raw number of persons selected for the job of laboratory technician from each of the sex and racial groups. To the right in column C (Number Applied) is the raw number of persons in each group who applied for the job of Laboratory Technician.

Analysis

Your task is to use the 80:20 rule to determine if there is adverse impact for any of the protected classes contained in this exercise. To do so, you must determine the selection rate--the Percentage Selected--for each group in column D of the output screen. As a result of these calculations, you will obtain a base rate--the selection rate of the group for which there is the highest selection rate. This base rate becomes the comparison rate. If there was no adverse impact, then the selection rates of other groups should not be less than 80% of the base rate.

Determining the Percentage Selected of the Number Who Applied. To accomplish this task, divide the raw number selected by the number who applied. For example, the entry in cell D13 is:

+B13/C13

Copy this formula to the remaining cells in column D for which there is a highlighted 0. (If you need help in copying a formula, review the section on Copying in Chapter 2.)

Column E (80% of Base Rate) must contain a figure which represents 80% of the highest (maximum) selection rate. Use a combination of the statistical function @MAX and a formula to calculate 80% of the highest selection rate. Move the cursor to cell E13 and type @MAX(. Then move the cursor to cell D13 to include the area for which you wish to find the highest number, and type a period. Next, move the cursor to cell D24 to include all of the selection rates, and type a right parenthesis so that Lotus 1-2-3 will move the cursor back to E13 with the following display at the top of the screen:

@MAX(D13..D24)

Now multiply the statistical function by .8 to complete the formula as follows:

$$@MAX(D13..D24)*.8$$

Lotus 1-2-3 will then find the highest selection rate in the designated area of column D, and it will multiply that rate by .8. Since you will need to compare this rate to the selection rates for all other groups, you will have to copy the entry in cell E13 to cells E14..E17 and E20..E24. Since you want the area of the worksheet in the @MAX statistical function to remain constant, you must edit cell E13 and change the cell addresses to absolute values before copying this cell. The change in cell D13 will result in its looking like the following:

$$@MAX(\$D\$13..\$D\$24)*.8$$

Determining the Existence or Nonexistence of Adverse Impact. Column F, labeled Adverse Impact, is designed to provide the answer to this task. A Lotus 1-2-3 formula that you may use to determine whether adverse impact exists is called a **logical operator**. The general form of the logical operator is:

$$@IF(logical\ value,\ value\ 1,\ value\ 2)$$

The logical function @IF always contains three arguments. The first argument--logical value--must be one which is either true or false. If the argument is true, then value 1 is entered in the cell in which this formula is entered; if it is false, then value 2 is entered in the cell.

A hypothetical example of the first argument follows:

$$@IF(A1<B1,$$

This expression of inequality may be either true or false; therefore, it appears to be an acceptable argument. If the value in cell A1 is less than the value in cell B1, the first argument is true. If the value in cell A1 is equal to or greater than the value in cell B1, the first argument is false.

The first argument of the logical function @IF may also contain the equal sign (=) or the "greater than" sign (>), depending on the type of the intended logical statement. By convention, the value for a true statement is one (1) and the value for a false statement is zero (0). Thus, you may complete the example about which you were just reading with the following:

$$@IF(A1<B1,1,0)$$

If you were to enter this formula in cell C1 and then copy it to cells C2 and C3 of the following Lotus 1-2-3 spreadsheet, you would obtain

81

these results:

	A	B	C
1	80	70	0
2	19	23	1
3	76	76	0

Cell C1 contains a zero (0) since 80 is not less than 70. In other words, the logical function (A1<B1) is false; therefore, the value indicating a false logical function (0) is entered in cell C1. By contrast, cell C2 contains a one (1) because 19 is less than 23. Since this is a true statement, a one (1) is entered appropriately in cell C2. Since 76 in cell A1 is equal to, not less than, 76 in cell B3, the entry in cell C3 is also a zero (0), indicating a false statement.

Your final task is to write a logical function @If for cell F13, which asks if the selection rate (Percentage Selected) for the group (D13) is less than the selection rate for the base rate (80% of Base Rate), E13. First, construct the inequality for the logical value. Second, use a one (1) for "yes" as the first value in the logical function and a zero (0) for "no" as the second value. Then copy this formula to cells F14..F17 and F20..F24.

Saving Your Worksheets

Save your work onto the Working Diskette by using the appropriate Lotus 1-2-3 File commands. (For assistance in using the File commands, consult Chapter 2.)

Printing the Results

After completing the information required for the output screen, print your results. Make sure that you edited cell A3 and typed your name into the cell after **Name:** and that you have returned the cursor to cell A1. Type /PP (PRINT PRINTER) to access the Lotus 1-2-3 print menu commands. Establish a print range by typing R (RANGE). Now enter the print range by typing the cell coordinates directly or type a period to indicate that A1 is the upper left coordinate. Then move the cursor to the right and down until you have included all of the output screen. Press the Enter key to store this information. Then proceed to print the results. (If you need assistance in printing the results, return to the section on Printing the Worksheets in Chapter 2.)

Analyzing the Results

You are now ready to evaluate whether there is adverse impact in the selection of staff nurses at Metro Hospital. In the space provided, answer the questions at the end of this chapter. Then tear out that page, attach it to the printed results, and turn both in to your instructor.

Endnotes

1. For more information about adverse impact, including nonquantitative definitions of adverse impact, see Arthur W. Sherman, Jr., George Bohlander, and Herbert J. Chruden, <u>Managing Human Resources</u>, Eighth Edition (Cincinnati, OH: South-Western Publishing Co., 1988).

2. Equal Employment Opportunity Commission, Civil Service Commission, Department of Labor, Department of Justice, "Adoption by Four Agencies of Uniform Guidelines on Employee Selection Procedures, <u>Federal Register</u>, Vol. 43, No. 166 (August 25, 1978), pp. 38290-38309.

Questions

1. Why is the base rate for the calculation of the 80% rule (four-fifths rule) the selection rate for White males?

2. For which protected groups is there adverse impact?

3. Explain how recruitment patterns may contribute to adverse impact.

4. What do you recommend as the next steps for the HR staff after having reviewed these data?

CHAPTER 8
TRAINING EMPLOYEES: BUILDING A TRAINING BUDGET

Lotus 1-2-3 applications in this chapter:

Command Menus
    FILE
    PRINT
Mathematical Operations
    Subtraction
    Multiplication
    Division
Statistical Functions
    @SUM
    @COUNT

Chapter Outline

Background of the Exercise
Retrieving TRAIN
Output Screen
Input Screen
Analysis
    Work Loss Expense
    Per Diem Allocation
    Budget for Each Item
    Budgeted Program Cost
    Summing the Cells
Saving Your Worksheets
Printing the Results
Analyzing the Results

With a HR Database, a HR department has a powerful tool for aiding departmental managers with their jobs. One area in which such aid can be provided is the management of a training budget.

Background of the Exercise

Metro Hospital allocates a training budget to some of its departments, and its upper management expects departmental managers to stay within their budgeted amount of training dollars.

To stay within the budget, Metro Hospital's HR Department offers managers help in setting up a small database to keep track of training expenditures. Rudy Pena, the Chief Medical Technician for the Medical Laboratory, requested such help because of the somewhat complicated system that Metro uses in its budget allocations. For example, Metro allocates a departmental expenditure for the cost of training programs equal to the number of people in the department multiplied by 2.25 times a day's instructional cost of $80. Both the $80 instructional cost and the 2.25 multiplier are derived from Metro's experience with training costs. These figures vary somewhat from department to department and are reviewed annually as the new fiscal year's budgets are established.

Per diem (expenses for food, hotel, etc. per day) and travel expenses are allocated similarly; the number of people in the department is multiplied by 2.25 times a budgeted amount. This year Metro is using a value of $75 for per diem and $100 for travel.

Metro Hospital also includes an allocation in the budget for the cost of lost work due to absence from the job. Metro Hospital managers believe that the lost work from having an employee in training is an expense associated with training, and they want to assure that there is some control of this expense. Metro uses a formula that assumes 22 work days per month (over 12 months), and it allocates the equivalent in total departmental salary of 2.25 days for the department's total salary budget. This amount is equivalent to an allocation of 2.25 days per employee multiplied by the employee's salary.

Naturally, Metro is not concerned about exactly spending the amount in each of the categories, but it is concerned with staying within the total budget as it is defined by summing the allocations for all of these categories. To aid Mr. Pena in monitoring his travel budget, a representative of the HR Department extracted several of the fields from the HR Database for all employees within the Medical Laboratory. Your tasks are to (1) enter the expenses that Mr. Pena anticipates will be associated with training in his department, and (2) build the necessary formulas for evaluating the relationship between the Medical Laboratory's training budget and anticipated expenses.

Retrieving TRAIN

Begin by retrieving the file called TRAIN from your HR Data Diskette. Then remove the HR Data Diskette from the computer's drive and replace it with your Working Diskette.

Output Screen

The output screen includes the cells A1..C20 (see Exhibit 8-1). It requires that you create the formulas for the budgeted amounts of the following:

1. Work Loss (the cost of lost work due to training days).
2. Program Cost.
3. Per Diem.
4. Travel (cost).

Exhibit 8-1

TRAIN
Training Employees: Building a Training Budget
Name:

OUTPUT SCREEN

Budget
   Work Loss $0
   Program Cost $0
   Per Diem $0
   Travel $0
Total Budget $0

Expenses
   Work Loss $0
   Program Cost $0
   Per Diem $0
   Travel $0
Total Expenses $0
Surplus(Deficit) $0

The section on Background of the Exercise in this chapter gives you the necessary information to build the formulas for each of these budgeted amounts. You will probably need to reread that section as you begin to develop the formulas.

The output screen also contains entries for the expenses associated with training in the department (cells A14..C19). Each of these cells in column C contains a cell entry from the input screen. As you review the input screen, you will see that column C cell entries refer to totals from the slice of the database used in this chapter.

Finally, the output screen also requires that you enter formulas for the Total Expenses (cells A19..A20) and the Surplus or Deficit associated with training (cells A20..C20).

Input Screen

The input screen, located in cells A24..M36, contains the following fields from the HR Database: Name (of the employee), Hire (date), Race, Sex, Job Title, Department, Salary, and Absences (days). In addition to these fields, columns within the worksheet area of I24..M36 have been added for the travel-related data associated with the Medical Laboratory. Cells in this area of the worksheet contain zeros, indicating data that you must supply to establish the necessary information for monitoring the travel budget (see Exhibits 8-2a and 8-2b).

Analysis

The first step in the analysis will be to enter the data supplied by Mr. Pena. These are his estimates of days of training, instructional cost of training, and travel cost.

Work Loss Expense. From the data supplied by Mr. Pena, calculate the work loss expense. First, enter these data in the appropriate columns of the worksheet, as follows:

Exhibit 8-2a

DATABASE

NAME	HIRE	RACE	SEX	JOB TITLE	DEPARTMENT	SALARY	ABSENCES	TRAINING DAYS	WORK LOSS EXPENSE
Abel, Judy	18-Apr-75	W	F	Histotechnician	MEDICAL LABORATORY	$18,394	16	0	$0
Abel, Sarah	12-Apr-76	W	F	Cytotechnician	MEDICAL LABORATORY	$15,723	31	0	$0
Cook, Jane	15-Nov-80	W	F	Cytotechnologist	MEDICAL LABORATORY	$22,379	7	0	$0
Criana, Lacy	15-Feb-81	W	F	Medical Technician	MEDICAL LABORATORY	$13,441	43	0	$0
Ferris, Michael	12-Jun-72	W	M	Medical Technician	MEDICAL LABORATORY	$16,352	14	0	$0
Pena, Rudy	01-Apr-65	H	M	Chief, Med Tech	MEDICAL LABORATORY	$33,127	0	0	$0
Ruch, Andrew	15-Oct-80	B	M	Medical Technologist	MEDICAL LABORATORY	$21,519	18	0	$0
Sampson, Marina	01-Sep-79	W	F	Medical Technologist	MEDICAL LABORATORY	$21,519	0	0	$0
Timms, Zelda	01-Mar-82	W	F	Histotechnician	MEDICAL LABORATORY	$13,978	23	0	$0
TOTAL						$176,432			$0

Exhibit 8-2b

PROGRAM COST	PER DIEM	COST OF TRAVEL
$0	$0	$0
$0	$0	$0
$0	$0	$0
$0	$0	$0
$0	$0	$0
$0	$0	$0
$0	$0	$0
$0	$0	$0
		$0
$0	$0	$0

	A	I	J	K	L	M
24		TRAINING	WORK LOSS	PROGRAM	PER	COST OF
25	EMPLOYEE	DAYS	EXPENSE	COST	DIEM	TRAVEL
26	Abel, J.	2		90		0
27	Abel, S.	0		0		0
28	Cook, J.	0		0		0
29	Criana, L.	6		370		516
30	Ferris, M.	3		225		218
31	Pena, R.	4		595		639
32	Ruch, A.	4		390		219
33	Sampson, M.	1		45		0
34	Timms, Z.	1		45		0

Second, calculate the cost of lost work based on Mr. Pena's estimate of the number of days of training for that employee. Since column J (Work Loss Expense) is a function of salary, develop a formula based on the yearly salary in column G. Of course, you will have to calculate the daily expense of this person's wages. The general form of the formula is:

(ANNUAL SALARY/(22 DAYS PER MONTH * 12 MONTHS))*TRAINING DAYS

Using your knowledge of Lotus 1-2-3, enter this formula in cell J26. (If you need assistance with the formula, consult the sections on Mathematical Operations and Formulas in Chapter 2.)

Finally, copy the formula to cells J27..J34. (If you need some help, consult the section on the Lotus 1-2-3 Copy command in Chapter 2.)

Per Diem Allocation. Since Metro pays a per diem rate of $75 per day for training days away from the hospital, calculate the reimbursement associated with per diem in column L by using the information in column I concerning the number of anticipated training days. The general form of the Lotus 1-2-3 formula for cell L26 is:

NUMBER OF DAYS OF TRAINING * $75

After typing this formula, copy it to the remaining cells in column L (i.e., cells L27..L34). Since the output screen calls for the total expenses associated with each of these fields, you will need to sum the values in columns J, K, L, and M. Cells J36..M36 contain highlighted zeroes, indicating the location in the worksheet for the Lotus 1-2-3 formulas required to sum each column. Recall that the statistical function @SUM takes the general form of:

@SUM(cellx..celly)

You may make this task considerably easier if you begin with cell J36. After entering the appropriate form of the statistical function @SUM

in this cell, copy it to the remaining highlighted zeros to its right. The
sums will be automatically entered in the output screen. Return to cell A1
and you will see that there are now entries for the Expenses.

Budget for Each Item. Your next task is to calculate the Budget for
each item in the output screen. Recall that the cost of lost work is calculated based on 2.25 days of the department's total salary budget. Metro
uses a formula that assumes 22 work days per month over 12 months. Thus,
the general form of this formula is:

$$(TOTAL\ SALARY/(22*12))*2.25$$

To calculate the cost of lost work, enter a formula in B8. To build
the formula, you will have to use the data from the input screen for the
sum of salaries of members of the department.

Budgeted Program Cost. Your next task is to calculate the budgeted
Program Cost, which is the cost of instruction. Recall that Metro allocates a departmental expenditure for the cost of training programs equal
to the number of people in the department multiplied by 2.25 times a day's
instructional cost of $80. To create a general formula which may be used
for other departments, use the statistical function @COUNT to build the
formula for B9. Begin by entering the following in cell B9:

@COUNT(

Then move the cursor to the name of the first employee in the Medical Laboratory and type a period. Next, move the cursor down to highlight
the names of the employees and type a right parenthesis. Lotus 1-2-3 will
return the cursor to cell B9 with the range of the names of the employees
in column A as a part of the statistical function @COUNT. Before pressing
the Enter key, complete the formula with multiplication signs, the 2.25
days, and the value of $80 per day, as follows:

*2.25*80

Per Diem in cell B10 and Travel Expense in cell B11 are calculated
very similarly to the formula that you just used to calculate Program
Cost. The differences lie in the base rates used. Per Diem uses a rate of
$75 per day for 2.25 days per employee in a department, and Travel uses a
rate of $100 per day for 2.25 days per employee in a department. Follow
the procedures outlined in the first paragraph of this section.

Summing the Cells. Your remaining tasks are (1) to sum cells
B8..B11 for the Total Budget entry in cell C12, (2) to sum Total Expenses
for the entry in cell C19, and (3) to calculate the Surplus or Deficit for
cell C20. In cells C12 and C19, use the statistical function @SUM; in cell
C20, subtract the total expenses from the total budget.

Saving Your Worksheets

Save your work onto the Working Diskette by using the appropriate Lotus 1-2-3 File commands. (For assistance in using the File commands, consult Chapter 2.)

Printing the Results

Before beginning to print the results, check to see that you have edited cell A3 and typed your name after the word **Name:**. Print the output screen by establishing a range of cells A1..C20. (You may seek assistance in printing the results by consulting the section on Lotus 1-2-3 Print Commands in Chapter 2.)

Analyzing the Results

You may now evaluate Mr. Pena's training budget for the Medical Laboratory. In the space provided, answer the questions at the end of this chapter. Then tear out that page, attach it to the printed results, and turn both in to your instructor.

Questions

1. Evaluate Mr. Pena's budget. Are his expenses reasonable, given what you know? What changes, if any, do you recommend?

2. Evaluate the appropriateness of including the expense of lost work due to absences as a part of a department's training budget. What are the advantages and disadvantages of doing this?

3. Given what you know about Metro's expenditures on training, its requirements for accountability of the departmental manager, etc., what assumptions do you believe Metro's upper management has made about training?

4. In what ways does a HR information system contribute to the ability of a department at Metro to manage its training budget?

CHAPTER 9
CAREER DEVELOPMENT

Lotus 1-2-3 applications in this chapter:

Command Menus
  FILE
  PRINT
Statistical Functions
  @COUNT
Database Statistical Functions
  @DCOUNT

Chapter Outline

Background of the Exercise
Retrieving CAREER
Three-Part Output Screen
Input Screen
Analysis
  Output Screen 1
  Output Screen 2
  Output Screen 3
Saving Your Worksheets
Printing the Results
Analyzing the Results

There are a variety of reasons for an organization to maintain an interest in the career development of its employees. Particularly important among those reasons is the role that career development plays in enhancing an employee's value to the organization. Enhancing the career development of employees provides the organization with anticipated skills. Furthermore, an emphasis on career development communicates an important message to employees: The organization values you. Communicating this message may well enhance employees' commitment to remain with the organization and lead them to put additional effort into their work.

Background of the Exercise

Underlying all the reasons for maintaining a career development program is the recognition of the value of human resources to the goal accomplishment of an organization. For these and other reasons, about a year ago Metro Hospital introduced a career development program for which the HR Department has responsibility.

The career development program consists of four elements, three of which were newly created. The initial element of the program was orientation, which Metro adopted in the early seventies and to which it had made many modifications since that time. The orientation program was included as a part of the general career development program because of its role in communicating information about the organization, including other aspects

99

of Metro's career development program. An additional reason for its inclusion was the belief of Metro managers that the orientation program contributes to the realistic job preview that enhances the satisfaction of employees and the probability of their retention.

The newly created three elements in the career development program are <u>career counseling, a periodic seminar on individual career development,</u> and the <u>career ladders</u> which the staff created for the various job families at Metro. At this time Metro contracts with an agency which provides counselors for employees who seek career counseling. Metro's HR staff has found that employees use the counselors for problems emanating from family and job. These problems include stress, substance abuse, career difficulties, etc. The career seminar is offered every three months, and the HR Department has contracted with a professor from the management department of a local college to teach this seminar. Career ladders are available for nearly all employees.

The career development program has been in effect for several months now, and the HR staff is concerned with evaluating it. As a preliminary step toward the evaluation of the program, the HR staff has decided to review the number and type of persons who are taking advantage of aspects of the program.

Retrieving CAREER

To aid the HR Department in this analysis, retrieve the file called CAREER from your data diskette. This file contains a slice of the HR Database with several of its fields, including the reported utilization of the various career program services. After retrieving CAREER, replace the HR Data Diskette with your Working Diskette.

Three-Part Output Screen

There are three Output Screens for this exercise (see Exhibit 9-1). Output Screen 1 includes cells A1..D22. This screen provides for two types of database searches: (1) summary data on the use of <u>all</u> career program services, and (2) summary data on the use of <u>any</u> of the career program services other than orientation.

Output Screen 2 is located in cells A23..G43. It provides more detailed information about those who have failed to attend the orientation program.

Output Screen 3 is located in cells A44..G91. It provides information that may be used in evaluating the use of the counseling service.

Exhibit 9-1

```
CAREER
Career Development
Name:

OUTPUT SCREEN 1 -  General Use

Criterion - Total Use
        ORIENTATION   COUNSEL   SEMINAR LADDER
              0           0         0     0


Number Employees         0
Use All Services         0


Criterion - Use Any Except Orientation
        ORIENTATION   COUNSEL   SEMINAR LADDER
                         0
                                   0
                                         0



Use Any Service          0
---------------------------------------------------------------------
Output Screen 2 -  No Orientation

Criterion - No Orientation
        ORIENTATION
                0

Output
        NAME           HIRE     BIRTH    RACE  SEX      DEPARTMENT




---------------------------------------------------------------------
Output Screen 3 -  Use of Counseling

Criterion - Use Counseling
      COUNSEL
                0

Output
        NAME           HIRE     BIRTH    RACE  SEX      JOB TITLE
```

Input Screen

The input screen, a slice of the HR Database used for this exercise, is located in cells A92..K215. It consists of the following fields: Name, Date of Hire, Date of Birth, Race, Sex, Job Title, Department, Career Orientation, Career Counsel, Career Seminar, and Career Ladder. Records contain a "Y" for "Yes" in the career program services fields if the employee has made use of the career service and a "N" for "No" if the employee has not made use of the service.

Analysis

After having reviewed the three output screens and the input screen, return the cursor to cell A1. As usual, supply information for those cells which contain a highlighted zero (0).

Output Screen 1. For Output Screen 1, you are interested in counting the number of employees who use all four career services. Before "creating the database," enter the correct code (Y for Yes or N for No) for use of a service beneath the field name for each service--cells A9..D9. By doing so, you will have entered the necessary information for establishing cells A8..D9 as the criterion for the database.

The entry in cell B11 is a count of the number of persons in the database. To count the records in the database (A95..K215), use the statistical function @COUNT. Cell B12 is a database count which employs the database statistical function @DCOUNT. The general form for this database statistical function is:

@DCOUNT(input,offset,criterion)

Notice that this command begins with the word @DCOUNT. Its name indicates that it is a counting function, but the word COUNT is preceded by the letter D, which stands for database. This function avoids the need to extract cases from a database and count the number of extracted cases.

The database statistical function @DCOUNT has three arguments. The first argument, Input, consists of all cells of the database in which the search will occur. For the four columns associated with the career program services (H94..K215), that area of the database consists of the field names and the data below the field names.

The second argument, Offset, is an integer. It indicates how many columns removed from the left-most column of the input range the function is to operate on. By indicating an offset of zero (0), the database statistical function will operate on the first column.

The final argument, Criterion, is the range of cells that includes the criterion name and the value below it for each of the four career program services (i.e., cells A8..D9).

102

To count the number of employees who have used all four career program services, enter the database statistical function in its specific form in cell B12. Remember to include the field names as a part of the input argument. Enter this function in cell B12 by starting with the following entry:

@DCOUNT (

Next, move the cursor to the appropriate part of the worksheet to include the input area of the database, and type a comma. This will return the cursor to cell B12 for the next part of the database statistical function, the offset. Typing a comma after the offset will once again allow you to move the cursor, but this time you will be highlighting the area of the criterion. Now type a right parenthesis, and Lotus 1-2-3 will return the cursor to B12 where you may enter the database statistical function.

Of interest to the HR Department staff is the number of employees who have used any one of the career program services other than the orientation program. To count those employees who have used any one service, Cells A15..D18 provide space in the worksheet for a criterion which will permit you to use the statistical function @DCOUNT. Note that the code for having used a service must be entered on a separate row for each service in cells A15..D18.

Entering the codes on the same row, as you just did in counting all of those who have used every service, results in Lotus 1-2-3's interpreting the criterion as if the word AND were entered between each field. That is, Lotus 1-2-3 interprets the single row of entries as stating that it is to extract records for those who have attended orientation and used career counseling and attended the career seminar and obtained information about the career ladder. By contrast, the use of entries on separate rows results in Lotus 1-2-3's interpreting the criterion as "Extract records for those employees who have used career counseling or attended the career seminar or obtained information about a career ladder."

After having entered the appropriate codes for the criterion in cells A16..D18, count the number of persons who have used any service other than orientation. The statistical function @DCOUNT should be entered in its appropriate form in cell B21. Copying the function from B12 will result in the wrong areas being identified. If you copy it from B12, you will have to edit it in order to change it. Perhaps you will find it easier to follow the same procedures you just used in entering the database statistical function @DCOUNT.

Output Screen 2. Move the cursor to A23 of Output Screen 2, which provides specific information about those who have failed to attend the orientation program, by extracting information about them. Since you are interested in those who have failed to attend the orientation program, enter the correct code in A27 for a negative response in the Orientation field of the database. Because you are going to extract information about

103

these employees rather than merely count them, you must "create a data-base." Begin by accessing the database query command menu of Lotus 1-2-3. (If you need assistance in using these Lotus 1-2-3 commands, you should review the section on Database Query Command in Chapter 2.)

Recall that you must establish the worksheet range of the input area (A94..K215), the criterion area (A26..A27), and the output area (A30..G41). Remember to include the field names as a part of each area which you establish with the database query commands. After entering the input range, the output range, and the criterion range, extract the cases that match the criterion by typing E (EXTRACT). If you have established the criterion, input, and output ranges correctly, the records of those employees who have not attended orientation will be listed in the area A30..G41.

Output Screen 3. The final analysis in this chapter extracts records of those employees who have used the career counseling service. The output screen for this analysis is located in cells A44..G88.

Begin by entering the appropriate value in cell A48 for a positive response to having used the counseling service. Access the database query command menu of Lotus 1-2-3 and reset the stored range values. After having established the worksheet ranges for the input, criterion, and the output, extract the cases that match the criterion from the database. When establishing a range for the output, use the cells A51..G88.

Saving Your Worksheets

Save your work onto the Working Diskette by using the appropriate Lotus 1-2-3 File commands. (For assistance in using the File commands, consult Chapter 2.)

Printing the Results

Before beginning to print the results, check to see that you have edited cell A3 and typed your name after the word **Name:**. Print Output Screens 1 and 2 by establishing a range of cells A1..E43. (You may seek assistance in printing the results by consulting the section on Lotus 1-2-3 Print Commands in Chapter 1.)

After printing Output Screens 1 and 2, reset the stored range values in the Lotus 1-2-3 print commands by typing CR (CLEAR RANGE) with the Lotus 1-2-3 print commands at the top of the screen. Now print Output Screen 3. Since your output extends beyond what is visible on the screen, you will need to use a border column for ease in reading the printed output. First, establish a range of B44..G88 and type OBC (OPTIONS BORDER COLUMNS). Then type A44 at the Lotus 1-2-3 prompt:

Enter Border Columns:A44

To leave this submenu and return to the main print menu, press the

Enter key, followed by Q (QUIT). You are now ready to print Output Screen
3.

Analyzing the Results

You may now evaluate the career development program which Metro Hospital has established. In the space provided, answer the questions at the end of this chapter. Then tear out that page, attach it to the printed results, and turn both in to your instructor.

Questions

1. How successful has the HR Department been in getting its employees to use the career program services?

2. How well is the HR Department doing in assuring that employees use the orientation program?

3. How successful has the HR Department been in getting its employees to use the career counseling program?

4. Evaluate Metro's career development program.

CHAPTER 10
APPRAISING AND IMPROVING PERFORMANCE:
A PEER RATING SYSTEM

Lotus 1-2-3 applications in this chapter:

Command Menus
   FILE
   PRINT
   COPY
Mathematical Operations
   Subtraction
   Multiplication
   Division
Statistical Functions
   @SUM
   @COUNT
   @AVG*
   @STD*
Database Statistical Function
   @DAVG*

Chapter Outline

Background of the Exercise
Retrieving PERF
Two-Part Output Screen
Input Screen
Analysis
   Output Screen 1
   Output Screen 2
Saving Your Worksheets
Printing the Results
Analyzing the Results

Performance appraisal is one of the major problems with which HR managers must deal. It is a problem because of the widespread dissatisfaction with appraisal methods that many companies are using.

_____

*Indicates a first-time use of this Lotus 1-2-3 application in this book.

Background of the Exercise

Dissatisfaction with appraisal methods has led the HR managers of Metro Hospital to investigate an alternative to their traditional appraisal method. Metro's traditional appraisal method for its managers included several performance rating scales, each of which was anchored with the adjectives "very poor" and "very superior". A value of one (1) was assigned to the lower end of the scale, and a value of seven (7) was assigned to the upper end of the scale. The scales were weighted with some values having greater importance than others. From the scores on each scale, a resulting weighted average was calculated and used to compare one manager to another for purposes of allocating merit pay. Accompanying this rating-scale method of evaluation was an assessment of the degree to which a manager had achieved previously established job-related objectives.

For some time the HR managers had recognized dissatisfaction with this appraisal method. Whereas there seemed to be general satisfaction with the job-related objectives section of the appraisal, there were complaints about the rating scale section. Some of the complaints centered on the difficulty of evaluating managers and other professionals. The complaints emanated from a feeling that managers and professionals are often involved with clients and other professionals in a way which limits their observation by the superiors who are doing the evaluating. Thus, evaluations are often distorted because they are affected by political tactics of the manager or professional rather than his/her performance.

Among the possible solutions to this problem was the use of peer ratings. There has been some discussion of peer ratings in the professional journals and books for HR managers. Unfortunately, the discussion has not been definitive in recommending for or against peer ratings.[1] Despite the mixed opinions and findings about peer ratings, the HR managers opted to give this approach a try. They decided to run a test with the line managers at the hospital. There was a feeling that the line managers' acceptance of this method would be critical to its ultimate adoption throughout the hospital.

The test of the peer-rating system included the following steps:

1. Managers were directed to choose five of their peers to evaluate them. Each of the chosen peers was asked to evaluate a manager on the same rating scales that had been previously used. Then the five peers' ratings were averaged.
2. At the same time, a manager's own superior was asked to use the same rating scales to conduct the usual evaluation that he/she completed. A comparison could then be made between the two ratings: the superior's rating and the peers' ratings.
3. An additional step was the collection of information about the relative satisfaction of participants with the new procedure. Each of the line managers was asked to indicate his/her agreement with the statement, The peer evaluation system provides

more accurate information about my performance than the managerial system, by checking one of the following responses:

          1 = Strongly Disagree
          2 = Disagree
          3 = Slightly Disagree
          4 = Slightly Agree
          5 = Agree
          6 = Strongly Agree

Your first task is to evaluate the appropriateness of using peer
ratings. While working with the performance ratings, the HR staff has another interest: Which of the head nurses to promote. This interest may be
satisfied by obtaining information from the HR Database.

Retrieving PERF

To evaluate the effectiveness of peer ratings and provide the neces-
sary information for making promotion decisions, retrieve the file called
PERF from your data diskette. Replace the HR Data Diskette with your
Working Diskette.

Two-Part Output Screen

There are two Output Screens for this exercise (see Exhibit 10-1).
Output Screen 1 is located in cells A1..B20. It requests information for
calculating a correlation coefficient between a manager's ratings of subordinate managers and the peers' ratings. A **correlation coefficient** is a
measure of the association between two sets of data. A high (approaching a
value of 1.0) positive correlation coefficient indicates that a manager's
rating and the peers' ratings are very similar. A correlation near zero
(0) suggests that there is little or no relationship between a superior's
rating and peers' ratings.

This output screen also requests a mean (average) rating on satisfaction with the peer-rating system. This mean rating will provide some
idea of how well those evaluated liked the peer-rating system.

Finally, Output Screen 1 requests a mean rating on satisfaction from
those who received a low rating from their peers. This information will
help determine whether a high or low satisfaction rating comes from the
process of using peer ratings or from the experience of having received a
high or low rating from one's peers.

Output Screen 2 is located in cells A21..I31 and allows you to extract information about the head nurses who should be considered for
promotion.

Exhibit 10-1

PERF
Appraising and Improving Performance: A Peer Rating Alternative
Name:

OUTPUT SCREEN 1

Rating Correlation:

Mean of Peer Rating	0.00
Mean of Manager Rating	0.00
Standard Dev. - Peer	0.00
Standard Dev. - Manager	0.00
Sum of Cross Products	0.00
Count of Managers (N)	0.00
Correlation Coefficient	0.00
Mean Satisfaction	0
Mean Satisfaction - Lo Rating	0.00

Criterion   PEER

OUTPUT SCREEN 2

Criterion   0

JOB TITLE   0

Selected Data

NAME	HIRE	BIRTH	RACE	SEX	JOB TITLE	DEPARTMENT	MANAGER MEAN

Input Screen

The input screen is located in cells A37..V64. You will observe that this slice of the HR Database includes the current weighted average performance appraisal ratings of the managers, called Rating Manager, and is located in cells N38..N64.

To test the peer-rating system, several additional fields were added to this slice of the database: the peer ratings (called PEER 1 through PEER 5 in cells O38..S64); the mean (average) of the five peer ratings (called PEER in cells T38..T64); the satisfaction measure (called SATIS-FACTION in cells U38..U64); and the cross products--the product of the manager's rating and the mean peer rating--(called PRODUCTS in cells V38..V64).

Analysis

To allay concerns of managers that their peers' evaluations may be very different from their superiors' evaluation, the HR staff decided to correlate the two ratings in order to see how similar they are. Several steps are necessary to generate the correlation coefficient--a measure of the relationship between the two sets of ratings.

Output Screen 1. Go to cell T38 of the input screen (the database). Using the function @AVG, calculate the mean of the five peer ratings for each manager in the database. This will result in replacing each of the zero entries in the T column below cell T39.

Begin by typing $@AVG($ in cell T40. Then move the cursor to O40. Type a period with the cursor at cell O40, move the cursor to S40, and type a right parenthesis. The cursor will automatically return to T40 where you should press the Enter key. After having calculated the mean peer rating for this manager, copy the statistical function to T41..T64.

Cell B9 requests a Mean of Peer Rating. This is a grand mean which requires that you once again use the statistical function @AVG. In this case, find the mean (average) of the entries in cells T40..T64 and enter that amount in cell B9. Follow the procedure which was just described for using the @AVG statistical function, but begin with the cursor in cell B9.

The Mean of Manager Rating (cell B10) is calculated in a similar manner. In this case the data for calculating the mean are in cells N40..N64. The statistical function for calculating the mean should be entered in cell B10.

Cells B11 and B12 require standard deviations. The **standard deviation** is a measure of the dispersion of the data. It is calculated with the following statistical function:

@STD(cellx..celly)

113

Cell B11 requires a standard deviation for the mean peer ratings (the data in cells T40..T64), and the entry in cell B12 should be a standard deviation of the data in cells N40..N64 (the standard deviation of a manager's rating of his/her subordinate manager).

Cell B13 requires the sum of the cross products. This calculation is a bit unusual; however, it is needed for the formula that you will use to calculate the correlation coefficient. Go to cell V38. Below the label in cells V38..V39, enter in cell V40 the formula for the product of the manager's rating (cell N40) and the mean peer rating (cell T40). In other words, enter in cell V40 the following formula for multiplying the manager's rating by the mean peer rating:

+N40*T40

Now copy this formula to cells V41..V64. Then return to cell B13 and enter the statistical function @SUM. Next, sum the cross products in cells V40..V64. Note that the sum of the cross products is an essential element for the correlation coefficient.

Before calculating the correlation coefficient, one additional entry is required. You will need to count the number of employees in the database--the N. At cell B14, enter the statistical function @COUNT, and count the number of employees from any column of the database (e.g., A40..A64).

As the word suggests, <u>correlation</u> is the interrelationship between sets of data. Here, it is the relationship between superiors' ratings of their subordinates and peers' ratings of one another. (If you are interested in the technical characteristics of a correlation coefficient, consult a basic textbook on statistics.)

From the calculations you have just completed, you can see that a correlation coefficient is composed of several important elements: the means of the sets of data, the sums of their cross products, their standard deviations, and the number of entries--the N. Here is a formula for the correlation coefficient:

$$((\text{sum of cross products}/N) - (\text{Mean}_1 * \text{Mean}_2)) / (\text{STD}_1 * \text{STD}_2)$$

This formula states that a correlation is the mean of the sum of the cross products minus the product of the two means, all of which is divided by the product of the standard deviations.

For cell B15, the formula is written as follows:

((B13/B14)-(B9*B10))/(B11*B12)

In addition to its interest in the relationship between the manager's evaluations and the peers' evaluations, the HR staff is interested in the degree of satisfaction with the peer ratings. Cell B16 calls for a mean of the data in cells U40..U64.

To gain additional insight into the relative satisfaction, the staff was curious about how those who were given low ratings reacted to the peer-rating system. Cell B17 requests a mean rating of the satisfaction scores for those who received low ratings. Below this cell is the database criterion for the variable PEER (i.e., the mean peer rating). Enter in cell B19 the following criterion formula for those persons with mean ratings below 5:

+T40<5

Notice that this formula uses the first cell below the label. This is typical of a formula used as a criterion in Lotus 1-2-3.

In cell B17, enter the following database statistical function for the mean (average) of the satisfaction scores for those who had mean peer ratings below 5:

@DAVG(T39..U64,1,B18..B19)

The first argument--T39..U64--defines the input area of the database. The second argument--1--calls for the U column to be searched. In other words, there is an offset of one column from the left of the input field. Finally, the third argument--B18..B19--establishes the location of the criterion in the worksheet.

Output Screen 2. Before leaving the managerial slice of the HR Database, you need to answer the question: Which of the head nurses should be considered for promotion? Since your task is to evaluate the head nurses, you will need to enter the job name--Head Nurse--in A25. To extract cases which match the job name from this slice of the HR Database, you will need to "create a database."

Begin by accessing the Lotus 1-2-3 database command menu and typing /DQ (DATA QUERY). Establish the input area, A39..V64, as the slice of the HR Database. Remember that you must include the single row of field names at the top of each column of the database. The output area should be cells A28..I31. The criterion area should include the field label and the job name. After "creating the database," you are ready to extract the information about the head nurses.

Saving Your Worksheets

Save your work onto the Working Diskette by using the appropriate Lotus 1-2-3 File commands. (For assistance in using the File commands, consult Chapter 2.)

Printing the Results

Before beginning to print the results, check to see that you have edited cell A3 and typed your name after the word **Name:**. Now print the results from Output Screen 1. Print only the section in the range A1..B20. (You may seek assistance in printing the results by consulting the section on Lotus 1-2-3 Print Commands in Chapter 2.) Then print Output Screen 2 in cells A21..I32.

Analyzing the Results

You may now evaluate the effectiveness of and satisfaction with the peer-rating system, as well as the qualifications of the head nurses. In the space provided, answer the questions at the end of this chapter. Then tear out that page, attach it to both sets of the printed results, and turn in all three items to your instructor.

Endnote

1. For a brief discussion of peer ratings, see R. I. Henderson, <u>Performance Appraisal</u>, 2d ed. (Reston, VA: Reston Publishing Co., 1984), pp. 33-37.

Questions

1. How similar is Metro Hospital's traditional rating method to the peer-rating system?

2. To what degree are the line managers satisfied with the peer-rating system? How does the actual peer rating affect their satisfaction with the system?

3. What can you recommend to Metro Hospital about the peer-rating system
    as a result of this test?

4. Whom do you recommend for promotion from among the head nurses?

CHAPTER 11
MOTIVATING EMPLOYEES: THE IMPORTANCE OF MONITORING
THE APPRAISAL PROCESS

Lotus 1-2-3 applications in this chapter:

Command Menus
   INSERT*
   FILE
   PRINT
   COPY
   DATA QUERY
   DATA SORT*
Mathematical Operations
   Subtraction
Statistical Functions
   @SUM
   @AVG
   @MAX
   @VAR*
   @MIN*

Chapter Outline

Background of the Exercise
Retrieving APPRSL
Output Screen
Input Screen
Analysis
   Timeliness of Appraisals
   Evidence of Rating Errors
Saving Your Worksheets
Printing the Results
Analyzing the Results

    Performance appraisal plays a critical role in motivating employees and improving their performance. It provides employees with information about their supervisors' expectations. If supervisors use a two-way communication style during appraisal discussions, employees have the opportunity to alert supervisors to the need for resources that may be lacking and are thus blocking their paths to effective performance.

---

    *Indicates a first-time use of this Lotus 1-2-3 application in this book.

Performance appraisal is also able to play a critical motivational role by enhancing employees' perceptions of the instrumental relationship between appropriate performance and organizational rewards. This motivational role is consistent with expectancy theory, one of the leading theories of motivation.[1]

If appraisal is to increase motivation, appraisal must take place. Actually getting supervisors to appraise employees is one of the difficulties that HR departments face. Whereas we know that supervisors should informally appraise employees frequently, practice as well as research tells us that appraisal occurs infrequently. Thus, one of the roles that many HR departments take on is assuring that at least one formal appraisal period occurs each year.

Not only must appraisal occur, but also supervisors must distinguish between levels of performance. They must distinguish between the poor performer and the good performer if they are to motivate excellent performance. Where global appraisal scales are used in the formal appraisal process, this need to differentiate the various levels of performance requires that supervisors avoid common rating errors.

Common rating errors include central tendency, positive rating bias, and negative rating bias. A **central tendency** rating error occurs when a supervisor rates everyone very close to the middle value on a rating scale. For example, a supervisor who rates all of his/her subordinates at 4 or 5 on a rating scale with a range of from 1 to 8 may be making this rating error. Of course, it is always possible that the performance of the employees is really average; thus, the rating may be acceptable and accurate rather than in error.

The second rating error is **positive rating bias**, which occurs when supervisors rate nearly all of their subordinates at the high end of the scale. A supervisor who falls prey to this rating error rates all of his/her employees at 7 or 8 on an 8-point scale on which 8 is the very best performance. This rating error is quite commonly made since supervisors like to provide good news rather than bad news to their subordinates.

Finally, a **negative rating bias** occurs when a supervisor rates most employees very poorly by rating them at the bottom of a scale--at 1, 2, or 3 on the same 8-point scale.

The problem that results from rating errors is inadequate feedback to employees. The feedback is poor because the supervisor makes very little distinction in his or her ratings. Thus, the feedback to a good performer appears very similar to the feedback a poorer performer receives. Very similar feedback means that appraisal has lost its ability to be punishing or reinforcing--important characteristics of effective feedback.[2] Moreover, the better-performing employees may believe that similar feedback is inequitable, and feelings of inequity damage the motivating character of the appraisal process.[3]

Background of the Exercise

Metro Hospital's HR Department has adopted several procedures to assure that appraisals occur and that rating errors are minimized. To assure that appraisals occur at least once each year, Metro has adopted the policy of appraising all employees on their hiring anniversary dates. To implement this policy, the HR Department notifies supervisors at least one month ahead of the anniversary date of an employee. The HR staff is trying to encourage supervisors to complete the formal appraisals prior to the anniversary date. Periodically, the HR staff reviews how well supervisors are doing in meeting the anniversary date deadline. When the staff reviews this information, it passes the information on to the supervisors' manager as well as to the supervisor himself or herself.

The HR Department also periodically reviews a supervisor's evaluations for rating errors. This review is done on the basis of the ratings on the global performance scale, which has values of 1 to 8, with 1 representing performance "substantially below expectations" and 8 representing performance "substantially above expectations." Usually the HR staff calculates a mean (average) score, a maximum, a minimum, and a variance.

The **mean score** provides information about the tendency of a supervisor to rate employees at the high, low, or middle range. For example, if the mean is a 7 relatively consistently, it is probable that there is positive rating bias.

The **minimum** and **maximum** values provide information about the degree to which the range is restricted (i.e., there is little variance in the supervisors' ratings). The range is calculated by subtracting the minimum from the maximum. A minimum and maximum which are very close together (e.g., a difference or range of 1 or 2 points) may suggest that the range of the evaluations is restricted. A restricted range provides very little difference in the feedback received by an excellent performer and a poor performer. The restricted range coupled with a mean in the middle of the range may suggest a rating error of central tendency as well.

Finally, the **variance** is a measure of dispersion or variation in the scores. It is related to the standard deviation, which you encountered in Chapter 10. It may be interpreted somewhat like the range. A small variance relative to the variance of other supervisors' ratings suggests restriction of range, which means undifferentiated feedback to the employees.

At this time, the HR Department has decided to review the supervisors' ratings and the timeliness of their ratings in the following departments: Security, Medical Laboratory, Emergency Room, and Accounting.

Retrieving APPRSL

To aid the staff with its analyses of the motivational qualities of the appraisal results in these departments, retrieve the file called AP-PRSL from your data diskette. This file contains a slice of the HR Database appropriate to the analyses in this chapter. Then replace the HR Data Diskette with your Working Diskette.

Output Screen

The output screen includes cells A1..G61 (see Exhibit 11-1). It contains the criterion labels upon which extractions from the database may be based. It also includes the area (below the word Output in cell A11) into which the extracted cases of the database may be written.

Input Screen

The input screen includes cells J6..P129. This slice of the database includes the following fields for each of the employees: Name, Job Title, Department, Yearly Absent (number of days absent), Appraisal Schedule (scheduled date for the appraisal), Appraisal Date (actual date of the appraisal), and Overall Score.

The last three (Appraisal Schedule, Appraisal Date, and Overall Score) are fields that you have not seen before. As with other field names, the portion of the field name which is used in database analyses is in the cell immediately above the data. The field Appraisal Schedule is the month and day of the employee's hiring anniversary. The field Appraisal Date is the month and day when the supervisor performed the appraisal. This date is derived from the appraisal form that the supervisor sends to the HR Department. The field Overall Score is a global rating with a range of 1 to 8, with 1 representing performance "substantially below expectations" and 8 representing performance "substantially above expectations."

Analysis

Your tasks are to evaluate the (1) timeliness of appraisals, and (2) the evidence of rating errors for four departments: Security, Medical Laboratory, Emergency Room, and Accounting. To accomplish these tasks, extract the relevant data for employees of the four departments. Enter the names of the four departments (exactly as they appear in the Database) beneath the criterion label DEPARTMENT. Since each department name is entered on a separate row, the criterion will be treated by Lotus 1-2-3 as if the word or were between each department name.

Exhibit 11-1

APPRSL
Motivating Employees: The Importance of Monitoring the Appraisal Process
Name:

Criterion

NAME	DEPARTMENT	ABSENT	SCHEDULE	DATE	TIMELY	SCORE

Output

NAME	DEPARTMENT	ABSENT	SCHEDULE	DATE	TIMELY	SCORE

Now you will need to "create a database." Recall that you may access the Lotus 1-2-3 database menu by typing /DQ (DATA QUERY). Begin by establishing the criterion as B6..B10. Establish the input and output areas of the spreadsheet. The output area is A12..G61, and the input area should include the field names and all of the employees in this slice of the database. (If you need assistance in "creating the database," review the section on Database Query Command in Chapter 2.) You are now ready to extract the cases that match the criterion.

If you still have the database menu at the top of the screen, press the Escape key several times or type Q (QUIT) to return to the Ready mode. To analyze the appraisals within each department, you will have to reorganize the extracted data by department. This task can be easily accomplished with the Sort command of Lotus 1-2-3. (If you need some assistance, review the section on Data Management in Chapter 2.)

With the Sort command menu at the top of the screen, type D (Data-Range) and move the cursor to cell A13. Notice that you will not include the field names in this range. You are only interested in sorting the employee records. Now type a period and move the cursor to the right and down to include all of the area in cells A13..G41. Press the Enter key to store this range.

To sort records with Lotus 1-2-3, you must establish the basis on which the sort will occur. This involves choosing the column or columns that will form the basis of the sort. Lotus 1-2-3 provides you with a <u>primary sort field</u> and a <u>secondary sort field</u>. For this sort, you will only need the primary sort field. Therefore, type P for Primary-Key. The Primary-Key command allows you to identify the column upon which data will be sorted.

Move the cursor to cell B13, the first entry under DEPARTMENT, and press the Enter key. You have identified this column as the basis for the sort. Lotus 1-2-3 will now ask whether you want the data sorted in ascending or descending order. By typing A and pressing the Enter key, you will identify ascending order. Thus, the data will be sorted in alphabetical order, beginning with A. Descending order will sort the data in alphabetical order, beginning with Z.

Type G for Go to begin the sort. The cases should now be reorganized with all of those in the Accounting Department at the top of the list and all of those in the Security Department at the bottom of the list.

Timeliness of Appraisals. The next step in the analysis is to evaluate the timeliness of the appraisals. You may have noted a column of the output area in which there are no data. This column, beginning at cell F12, is called Timely. It contains no data because this field name is not a part of the larger database. Thus, no data could have been extracted for this column of the output area. This column requires a formula that will provide an indication of the timeliness of the appraisals. The formula will subtract the date of the scheduled appraisal from the date of the actual appraisal. Since Lotus 1-2-3 stores dates as a single number, this type of calculation may be performed.

In cell F13, enter a formula that subtracts the date in cell D13 from the date in cell E13. Copy this formula to the remaining cells in column F for which there is an extracted case. A zero indicates that the appraisal was done exactly on the anniversary date. A positive number indicates that the appraisal date was late since a later date is stored as a larger number and you subtracted a smaller number from this larger number. A negative number indicates that the appraisal occurred prior to the scheduled date.

Although you can get some idea of how well a supervisor is doing by merely scanning the entries below the field Timely, you can obtain a summary index number for each department being analyzed. That index is merely the sum of the entries in this column for each department. To obtain this sum, you will need to provide some space between each department's records. Lotus 1-2-3 allows you to do this by inserting rows. Move the cursor to cell F22. This cell is in the row below the last case from the Accounting Department. Type /WI (WORKSHEET INSERT), and the submenu will allow you to select a column or row for insertion. Type R for Row, and move the cursor down four rows to cell F26. Now press the Enter key, and Lotus 1-2-3 will insert five rows below the last case from the Accounting Department. You will need to follow the same procedure for entering five rows below the cases from the Emergency Room and the Medical Laboratory. Remember to begin by moving the cursor to one of the cells in the row just below the last case from a department.

After having inserted rows between each department, return to cell F22 and enter the formula for summing the numbers in cells F13..F21 to obtain the summary index mentioned earlier. Use the statistical function @Sum to perform this calculation. After completing it for the Accounting Department, do the same for each of the remaining departments by entering similar formulas in column F just below the last case from each department. To identify these results for someone else, you may call them Sum. Enter the word Sum in the cell just to the left of the formula for each department (e.g., in cell E22 for the Accounting Department).

Evidence of Rating Errors. Below the word Sum for each department, type Mean, Max, Min, and Var on separate rows in column E. You may now enter the formulas in column G that will provide information about rating errors. This information includes the mean (average) overall score, the maximum score, the minimum score, and the variance (a measure of the dispersion of the data) of the overall appraisal scores. Remember that you are interested in computing these formulas for the data in column G--i.e., the appraisal scores. Thus, you will enter these formulas in the cells of column G to the right of the labels in column E. This procedure contrasts with the @SUM formula which was entered in column F. In column G (and in the cell one column over to the right of each of these labels), enter the formulas for calculating the mean, maximum, minimum, and the variance. For example, in cell G23 type the following formula for calculating the mean of a series of numbers using the Lotus 1-2-3 statistical function @AVG:

@AVG(G13..G21)

Use the statistical function @MAX in cell G24 to locate the maximum value of the same series:

@MAX(G13..G21)

Similarly, enter the statistical function @MIN in cell G25 to locate the minimum value of the following series:

@MIN(G13..G21)

Finally, enter the following statistical function @VAR in cell G26:

@VAR(G13..G21)

After having completed these calculations, you will have the information that you need to evaluate the degree to which there are rating errors on the part of the manager of this department. Follow the procedures just described; enter the labels and statistical functions for each of the three remaining departments to evaluate the timeliness of the appraisals and rating errors of these managers.

Saving Your Worksheets

Save your work onto the Working Diskette by using the appropriate Lotus 1-2-3 File commands. (For assistance in using the File commands, consult Chapter 2.)

Printing the Results

Before beginning to print the results, check to see that you have edited cell A3 and typed your name after the word **Name:**. Print the output screen by establishing a range of cells A1..G61. (You may seek assistance in printing the results by consulting the section on Lotus 1-2-3 Print Commands in Chapter 2.)

Analyzing the Results

You may now evaluate the timeliness of the appraisals and the supervisors' rating errors from these selected departments. From these data you will be able to make some inferences about the motivating potential of the appraisal process from one department to another. In the space provided, answer the questions at the end of this chapter. Then tear out that page, attach it to the printed results, and turn both in to your instructor.

Endnotes

1. General information about motivation is available in Arthur W. Sherman, Jr., George Bohlander, and Herbert J. Chruden, <u>Managing Human Resources</u>, Eighth Edition (Cincinnati, OH: South-Western Publishing Co., 1988); specific information about expectancy theory is provided in Victor H. Vroom, <u>Work and Motivation</u> (New York: John Wiley & Sons, 1964), p. 170.

2. Frederick Luthans and Robert Kreitner, <u>Organizational Behavior Modification and Beyond: An Operant and Social Learning Approach</u>, Second Edition (Glenview, IL: Scott, Foresman, 1985).

3. S. Adams, "Inequity in Social Exchange," <u>Advances in Experimental Social Psychology</u>, edited by L. Berkowitz (New York: Academic Press, 1965), pp. 276-299.

Questions

1. How well are managers doing in completing their appraisals on time?

2. What, if any, action is required from the HR staff?

3. Identify any possible examples of rating error, including central
    tendency, positive rating bias, negative rating bias, and restricted
    range. What evidence do you have of these errors?

4. What steps should the HR staff take in dealing with rating errors?

CHAPTER 12
FACILITATING COMMUNICATION

Lotus 1-2-3 applications in this chapter:

Command Menus
 FILE
 PRINT
 DATA QUERY
 DATA SORT
Statistical Functions
 @AVG

Chapter Outline

Background of the Exercise
Retrieving COM
Output Screen
Input Screen
Analysis
Saving Your Worksheets
Printing the Results
Analyzing the Results

The focus of many recent discussions of effective management has been on the need for dynamic leadership. Without dynamic leadership, managers become little more than administrators who process the paperwork associated with their jobs. Such administrators are unable to provide the creative direction that differentiates a truly excellent organization from its competitors.

This focus on leadership has led managers to consider the elements of leadership that contribute to its effectiveness. One of those elements is the communication behavior of a manager with his/ her subordinates. Charles Redding, a noted communication scholar, described effective leaders as (1) more communication-oriented and more likely to speak up, (2) more receptive and responsive to subordinate inquiries, (3) more likely to ask or persuade rather than tell, and (4) more likely to give advance notice of changes--that is, communicate more openly.[1]

From this perspective, it is clear that the relational messages of <u>receptiveness</u> and <u>responsiveness</u> are important aspects of the leader's communication behavior. In addition to the relational messages of receptiveness and responsiveness, Penley and Hawkins identified four specific content-oriented types of communication that are necessary for effective leadership: performance communication, task communication, career communication, and personal communication.[2] In their research, they concluded that managers who wish to provide structure for their subordinates should frequently communicate messages associated with task assignment as well as provide information about the degree to which the subordinates' performance is effective.

Demonstrating concern for subordinates depends not only upon the relational messages of responsiveness, but also on providing the subordinates with information about what needs to be done--task communication. Moreover, leaders who were perceived as demonstrating concern for their subordinates and providing task structure were those managers who also provided their subordinates with career guidance.

Background of the Exercise

The Director of Metro Hospital was aware of the Penley-Hawkins research which demonstrated the importance of effective communication to effective leadership. One of his goals was to improve the leadership of his managers through their communication behavior. The Director decided to provide training and counseling for managers who needed to improve their communication. As a preliminary step to providing this training, the Director surveyed the communication effectiveness of departmental managers as perceived by their subordinates.

The survey, conducted by Metro's HR staff, used the communication questionnaire which Penley and Hawkins developed in their research. The HR staff surveyed only nonsupervisory personnel on the 19 items from the communication questionnaire which provides measures on five communication scales: (1) performance communication, (2) task communication, (3) career communication, (4) personal communication, and (5) responsiveness.

The **performance communication scale** measures the extent to which supervisors communicate information about the quality of subordinates' work or how well they are doing. The **task communication scale** measures the extent to which supervisors tell subordinates what needs to be done and explain policy and changes in the work place. The **career communication** scale is concerned with the degree to which supervisors and subordinates discuss the subordinates' training needs and career direction. The **personal communication scale** is concerned with the extent to which supervisors take the time to discuss personal topics with subordinates. Finally, the **responsiveness scale** measures the extent to which supervisors listen to subordinates and respond to their concerns. For each scale, the scale values range from 1 to 6, with 1 representing the poorest communication and 6 representing the best communication.

Of particular concern to the Director of the Hospital was the effectiveness of communication among the nursing staff. Therefore, the HR staff decided to first analyze the results of the communication survey from the nursing staffs of four departments: Surgical Recovery, Pediatrics, Orthopedics, and OBGYN. Your task is to determine the extent to which subordinates in these departments perceive the communication behavior of their supervisors as typical of dynamic leadership.

Retrieving COM

Retrieve the Lotus 1-2-3 file called COM from your HR Data Diskette.

Then replace the HR Data Diskette with your Working Diskette.

Output Screen

The output screen for this exercise covers cells A1..H56 (see Exhibits 12-1a and 12-1b). This area includes the mean scores on the communication scales that should be calculated and the criterion and output area for the database queries associated with the four departments in which you are interested.

Input Screen

The input screen consists of a slice of the HR Database covering cells A62..H161. This area contains only nonsupervisory personnel and information in the following database fields: Name, Job Title, and Department. Accompanying this slice of the database are scale scores on the five communication scales: Performance Communication, Task Communication, Career Communication, Personal Communication, and Communication Responsiveness.

Analysis

To begin your analysis, calculate the overall means (Grand Means) for each of the scales by using the Lotus 1-2-3 statistical function @AVG. As the argument for the statistical function @AVG, use the range of the worksheet area in which the data are located (i.e., the slice of the HR database from the input screen). Enter the statistical functions in cells B9..B13. (If you need assistance with the statistical function @AVG, consult the section on Statistical Functions in Chapter 2.)

To compare the grand means to the departmental means, extract data for the four departments. Move the cursor to cell A17. You will see on your screen that the criterion for the database query is already entered. Under the label DEPARTMENT are the four departments in which you are interested. Below row 24 is the area for the output of the database query.

Create the database. The input is the database itself. As you establish the input area, be sure to include the field names at the top of each column as the first row in the input area. The criterion includes the label DEPARTMENT in cell A18 and the four cells below it. Since each department name is on a separate row of the worksheet, Lotus 1-2-3 selects employees who are in any of the four listed departments. The output area for this database query is A25..H49. After creating the database, extract the cases which match the criterion.

You now have the data that you will need for the remainder of your analyses, but you will need to organize them by department. You can do this by sorting the data. If you still have the Lotus 1-2-3 database command menu at the top of the screen, type Q for Quit.

Exhibit 12-1a

COM
Facilitating Communication
Name:

OUTPUT SCREEN

SCALES	GRAND MEANS	SURGICAL RECOVERY	PEDIATRICS	ORTHOPEDICS	OBGYN	SCALES
Performance	0.00	0.00	0.00	0.00	0.00	Performance
Task	0.00	0.00	0.00	0.00	0.00	Task
Career	0.00	0.00	0.00	0.00	0.00	Career
Personal	0.00	0.00	0.00	0.00	0.00	Personal
Responsiveness	0.00	0.00	0.00	0.00	0.00	Responsiveness

Criterion
DEPARTMENT
SURGICAL RECOVERY
PEDIATRICS
ORTHOPEDICS
OBGYN

Output

NAME	JOB TITLE	DEPARTMENT	PERFORMANCE	TASK	CAREER	PERSONAL	RESPONSIVENESS

Exhibit 12-1b

OUTPUT SCREEN 4
Pay More Than $200
CRITERION

NAME	AGE	SEX	BELOW 7	USE	PAY
					0

QUERY OUTPUT

NAME	AGE	SEX	BELOW 7	USE	PAY

TOTAL COUNT   0
NUMBER OF CHILDREN   0

Sort the employee records by department. Use descending order for the sort. When you establish the Data-Range, be sure to enter the range only for the records and not the field names. (If you need assistance in sorting the data, consult the subsection on Sort Commands in Chapter 2.)

You will find that it is easier to calculate the means for each of the departments if there are rows between the records which come from different departments. You can do this by moving the cursor to cell C30, which contains the first employee record in the Pediatrics Department. Move the cursor to C30. To insert a row, type /WIR (WORKSHEET INSERT ROW). At the following Lotus 1-2-3 request:

Enter row insert range:C30..C30

press the Enter key. You now should have a row between the employee records from the Surgical Recovery Department and the employee records from the Pediatrics Department. Repeat this procedure for inserting a row between each of the remaining departments.

If you make a mistake and insert a row at the wrong place, move the cursor to a blank cell within the incorrect row and type /WDR (WORKSHEET DELETE ROW). At the following Lotus 1-2-3 prompt:

Enter range of rows to delete:

press the Enter key to delete the row at which the cursor is positioned. Continue by inserting the row at its proper place between the records coming from different departments.

Now return to cell C7 to begin the process of calculating the means for each department on all five communication scales. Move the cursor until the worksheet area C7..G13 is visible on the screen. Notice that the names of the scales have been duplicated in G8..G13. In cell C9, enter the Lotus 1-2-3 statistical function @AVG to calculate the Performance Communication mean for the Surgical Recovery Department. As the argument for the statistical function @AVG, use the range of data which you extracted from the database. Complete the output screen in C7..G13 by calculating mean scores on each of the communication scales for each of the four departments.

Saving Your Worksheets

Save your work onto the Working Diskette by using the appropriate Lotus 1-2-3 File commands. (For assistance in using the File commands, consult Chapter 2.)

Printing the Results

Before beginning to print the results, check to see that you have edited cell A3 and typed your name after the word **Name:**. Print the output screen by establishing a range of B1..F13. Since the range will require more than one page, a left border will aid the reader in understanding the data. Therefore, type /PP (PRINT PRINTER) and type OBC (OPTIONS BORDER COLUMN). At the following request:

Enter Border Columns:

type A1 for the A column. Press the Enter key. To leave this Options sub-menu, type Q (QUIT) and continue by printing the results. (You may seek assistance in printing the results by consulting the section on Lotus 1-2-3 Print Commands in Chapter 2.)

Analyzing the Results

You may now evaluate the degree to which leadership-related communication is effective. In the space provided, answer the questions at the end of this chapter. Then tear out that page, attach it to the printed results, and turn both in to your instructor.

Endnotes

1. W. Charles Redding, "Human Communication Behavior in Complex Organizations: Some Fallacies Revisited," in C. E. Larson and F. E. X. Dance (Eds.), <u>Perspectiveness on Communication</u> (Milwaukee: Speech Communication Center, University of Wisconsin-Milwaukee, 1968).

2. Larry E. Penley and Brian Hawkins, "Studying Interpersonal Communication in Organizations: A Leadership Application," <u>Academy of Management Journal</u>, 28 (1985), 309-326.

Questions

1. Analyze the four departments in terms of their leadership communication.

    a. In which departments do there appear to be problems with communication?

    b. In which departments are employees most satisfied with the communication?

2. In the department(s) for which communication appears weak, is there any pattern that explains the communication behavior?

3. What recommendations can you make for Metro Hospital's communication training program?

CHAPTER 13
COLLECTIVE BARGAINING AND CONTRACT ADMINISTRATION

Lotus 1-2-3 applications in this chapter:

Command Menus
   FILE
   PRINT
   COPY
Mathematical Operations
   Addition*
   Subtraction
   Multiplication
   Division
Statistical Functions
   @SUM
Special Functions
   @VLOOKUP*

Chapter Outline

Background of the Exercise
Retrieving LABOR
Output Screen
Input Screen
Analysis
Saving Your Worksheets
Printing the Results
Analyzing the Results

Along with other areas of the service sector, hospitals have been a target for unionization in the seventies and eighties. Although the first examples of unionization of the health-care industry may be traced to San Francisco in the pre-Depression period, the 1974 lifting of the Taft-Hartley exclusion from the federal collective bargaining laws, with amendments to the National Labor Relations Act, gave impetus to the unionization of the health-care industry.

Due to the critical nature of health care and the disruption that results from a strike in this industry, special collective bargaining provisions were established for the industry in Congress's 1974 health-care amendments. One of the purposes of these special provisions is to provide the health-care institution sufficient time to make alternative arrangements prior to any work stoppage.[1] The provisions include:

_____

   *Indicates a first-time use of this Lotus 1-2-3 application in this book.

1. A party wishing to change an aspect of the existing contract must notify the other party 90 days prior to the expiration of the agreement. Neither party may strike nor lock out until the contract expires or the 90 days end, whichever is later.
2. Within 30 days after issuing the first notice, the initiating party must notify the Federal Mediation and Conciliation Service (FMCS) of the existence of a dispute.
3. Mediation by FMCS is mandatory in order to reduce the risk of a strike or lockout.
4. The Director of FMCS may appoint a fact-finding board of inquiry 30 days prior to the contract administration.
5. If neither mediation nor the recommendations of the board of inquiry resolve the differences between the parties, the employee organization is required to notify management in writing of the intention to strike ten days prior to the strike.

In addition to these special rules for the health-care industry, there are other collective bargaining distinctions associated with this industry. One of those is the restriction that has emerged on the number of bargaining units within an institution.[2] A **bargaining unit** is the group of employees covered by a labor agreement. Congress recognized the negative impact of a large number of bargaining units on the operations of a hospital. Fragmentation of bargaining units can result in conflict and rivalry among the employee groups represented as different bargaining units. As a result of Congressional intent and subsequent National Labor Relations Board cases, there has been general recognition of six bargaining units within a hospital representing the following categories of employees: (1) nurses, (2) physicians, (3) other professionals, (4) clerical employees, (5) technical employees, and (6) service and maintenance employees.

Background of the Exercise

Metro Hospital has just received the required 90 days' notification of disagreement with certain provisions of the expiring contract from the representative of the <u>technical employees</u> bargaining unit. Among the proposals of the bargaining unit's representative are the following:

1. Provide two weeks' vacation to employees with from one to three years of tenure (time on the job at Metro).
2. Provide three weeks' vacation to employees with from four to eight years of tenure.
3. Provide four weeks' vacation to employees with over eight years of tenure.
4. Employ a hospital counselor to aid the employees in dealing with crises such as divorce, substance abuse, and family problems.

At this time Metro Hospital offers a one-week vacation to employees with from one to two years of tenure, and it offers two weeks' vacation to all employees with three or more years of tenure. No counselor for the employees is employed at this time. The hospital management's negotiating team recognizes that its vacation policy is somewhat limited when compared with other employers in the labor market area. Even when compared to other health-care facilities, Metro's vacation policy may be on the low side. Still, vacation costs can be expensive, and any increases in vacation for the technical employees' bargaining unit is likely to make an impact on negotiations with the other bargaining units.

The negotiating team also recognizes legitimate demands for counseling support, particularly for substance abuse problems and personality disorders. The team doubts that a counselor will be able to handle the personality disorders that have sometimes represented limited but severe problems in managing selected employees.

As a result of these considerations, one member of the negotiating team made the following suggestions as a counteroffer for mediation:

1. Provide one week's vacation to employees with from one to two years of tenure.
2. Provide two weeks' vacation to employees with from three to five years of tenure.
3. Provide three weeks' vacation to employees with from six to ten years of tenure.
4. Provide four weeks' vacation to employees with more than ten years of tenure.
5. Provide employees with the addition of psychiatric health care insurance coverage at a cost of $10.00 per month per employee.
6. Contract with a counseling service for counseling at $50 per hour, with a maximum of 16 weeks of weekly one-hour sessions of counseling per employee. Offer this service to employees upon a supervisor's recommendation to the HR department.

To evaluate the union's proposal as well as the impact of the suggested counteroffer, the negotiating team asked the HR staff to calculate the costs of the bargaining unit's proposal and the costs of the suggested counteroffer.

Retrieving LABOR

Retrieve the file called LABOR from your data diskette. This file is a slice of the database representing the technical employees who form this bargaining unit. Then replace the HR Data Diskette with the Working Diskette.

Output Screen

The output screen covers cells A1..D39 (see Exhibit 13-1). In column A are the labels for the following items that must be calculated: Cost of Vacation (current), Proposal Cost, Offer (counteroffer) Cost, Expense (Savings) of the Proposal or Offer, Cost of Health and Dental Plan (current), Counselor (projected cost of), Cost of Psychiatric (insurance coverage), Hourly Counseling (cost), and Total Additional Expense (of the proposal and the suggested counteroffer). Columns C and D will contain the calculated values for these labels, with column C representing the Additional Expense of the Proposal and column D representing the Additional Expense of the Counteroffer.

The worksheet area A21..D39 (Vacation Table) is called an index table. It is the basis for calculating the number of vacation hours per year to which each employee is entitled. Entitlement is based on the number of years of tenure with Metro Hospital. For example, an employee with one year of service is entitled to 40 hours of vacation time under the current contract. An employee with three years of service is entitled to 80 hours of vacation time. As you review the input screen, you will see how this table is used in calculating vacation expenses.

Input Screen

The slice of the HR Database used in this exercise covers cells A48..R82. The fields included in this screen are: Name (of the employee), Date of Hire, Date of Birth, Race, Sex, Job Title, Department, Annual Salary, Tenure, Vacation (number of hours), Insurance Health (cost), and Insurance Dental (cost).

The number of hours of vacation in column J is calculated using the vacation table (cells A21..D39) of the output screen. The @VLOOKUP special function is used to calculate vacation. It will be explained later in the chapter.

Columns K, L, M, N, O, and R are fields that have been added to this slice of the database to make the necessary calculations for evaluating the proposal and counteroffer. Those fields include the following: Vacation Cost (of the current vacation plan), Vacation Proposal (number of hours), Vacation Cost$_2$ (cost of the proposal), Vacation Offer (amount of vacation allocated to employees in the suggested counteroffer), Vacation Cost$_3$ (cost of the counteroffer), and Insurance Psychiatric (cost of psychiatric insurance).

Exhibit 13-1

LABOR
Collective Bargaining and Contract Administration
Name:

OUTPUT

		Additional Expense	
		of Proposal	of Offer
Cost of Vacation =	$0.00		
Proposal Cost =	$0.00		
Offer Cost =	$0.00		
Expense(Savings) =		$0.00	$0.00
Cost of Health/Dental =	$0.00		
Counselor =		$37,200.00	
Cost of Psychiatric =			$0.00
Hourly Counseling =			$0.00
Total Additional Expense		$0.00	$0.00

VACATION TABLE

Service Years	Vacation	Proposed Vacation	Offered Vacation
0	0	0	0
1	40	0	0
2	40	0	0
3	80	0	0
4	80	0	0
5	80	0	0
6	80	0	0
7	80	0	0
8	80	0	0
9	80	0	0
10	80	0	0
11	80	0	0
12	80	0	0
13	80	0	0
14	80	0	0
15	80	0	0

Analysis

Your first step in analyzing the costs of the union's proposal and the counteroffer is to calculate the cost of vacation under the current plan. Recall from the index table (A21..D39) that employees with from one to two years of tenure receive one week's vacation (or 40 hours) and that employees with three or more years of service receive two weeks' vacation (or 80 hours).

Move the cursor to cell J50 where you will see the number of hours of vacation received by employees in the current plan. In cell J51, you will see how vacation was calculated from the index table. The special function, @VLOOKUP, was used. This type of Lotus 1-2-3 special function allows the user to select a particular item from an index table based on the argument contained in the function. The general form of this special function is:

@VLOOKUP (argument, table range, column number)

@VLOOKUP is a vertical table lookup that uses the <u>argument</u> as the basis for choosing the cell in the first vertical index column of the table. The table's location in the worksheet is defined by the <u>table range</u>, the second item within the parenthetical expression of @VLOOKUP. After having located the row based on the <u>argument</u>, @VLOOKUP then moves over the number of columns identified by the <u>column number</u>, the third item in the parenthetical expression.

Note that the entry in cell J51 reads as follows:

@VLOOKUP (I51,$A$24..$D$39,1)

This form of the @VLOOKUP special function tells Lotus 1-2-3 to go to the table located in the worksheet area, A24..D39. Since the dollar signs are used before and after the column letter, these cell addresses are absolute and will not be changed as this function is copied to other locations in the worksheet.

The first entry in the parenthetical expression, the argument, tells Lotus 1-2-3 to use the value located in cell I51 as the particular row of the index column in which to search. Column I of the database is labeled Tenure, and it contains the number of years of service at Metro Hospital. The values in column I are calculated with the following formula which you may observe in cell I51:

(@TODAY-B51)/365

Cell B51 contains the Date of Hire; thus, this formula calculates the current tenure of each employee by subtracting the Date of Hire from today's date. This value will vary depending on the date which was entered when you started your computer. If 11 were the value in cell I51, @VLOOKUP would move down the index column, beginning at A24, until it reaches a number greater than 11. Lotus 1-2-3 would then return to the previous cell which contains 11.

The column number, one (1), tells Lotus 1-2-3 to search the first column to the right of the index column where the number of hours of allocated vacation are stored, using the current plan. (A two (2) would have resulted in Lotus 1-2-3's searching the second column to the right of the index column.) Since the number to the right of 11 in column 1 is 80 (hours of vacation time), cell J51 will contain the number 80 from the table at A24..D39.

You may wish to review the calculations of vacation hours in column J for several other employees to assure yourself that you understand the use of the Lotus 1-2-3 special function @VLOOKUP.

Before leaving this section of the worksheet, notice that column K contains the cost of vacation for each employee based on the existing allocation of vacation hours. The cost of vacation for each employee was calculated as follows, and cell K51 provides an example of this type of calculation:

(Annual Salary/52 Weeks/40 Hours) * Vacation Hours

Return to cell A1 (Home). Notice that the first highlighted zero is for the cost of vacation (based on the current plan). Calculate the total cost of vacation according to the current plan by summing the individual costs in column K (K51..K82) of the database. Enter the appropriate Lotus 1-2-3 statistical function with the required range in B8.

To calculate the costs of the union's proposal and the counteroffer (B9 and B10 in the output screen), first complete the index table in the output screen. Move the cursor to cell A21. Based on the description of the proposal provided earlier in this chapter, enter in the table the number of hours of vacation which correspond to each of the years of service.

After completing this task for the union's proposal, complete the corresponding task for the suggested counteroffer using the information that was also supplied earlier. With the table complete, you are now ready to calculate the vacation hours and associated costs for the union's proposal and the counteroffer.

Go to L51. In cell L51, enter the special function @VLOOKUP for calculating vacation from the table entries associated with the union's proposal. The function looks very similar to the one used in cell J51; however, the column entry will have to be two (2) since you are asking Lotus 1-2-3 to look in the second column of the vacation table for the entry. To count the years of service, you will still want Lotus 1-2-3 to use the information in column I of the database under the label Tenure. Thus, the function in cell L51 should look like this:

After entering this formula in cell L51, copy it to the remainder of the records in column L.

Column M is provided for calculating the cost of vacation associated with the proposal. Calculate the cost as you did in column K; however, use the number of hours of vacation in column L as a part of the formula for the calculated cost.

Complete a similar set of calculations for the suggested counteroffer in columns N and O of the database. Column N provides the cells with highlighted zeros for calculating the number of hours of vacation using the Lotus 1-2-3 special function @VLOOKUP. Column O provides the cells for calculating the cost of vacation for each employee. Then return to the output screen.

Cell B9 is the sum of the vacation costs for each employee if the union's proposal were adopted. To add the entries in column M (M51..M82), use the appropriate Lotus 1-2-3 statistical function. In cell B10, follow this procedure for calculating the cost of the suggested counteroffer.

The entry in cell C11 is the additional expense of the proposal, and it may be calculated by subtracting the cost of employee vacations associated with the current plan from the cost of the union's proposal. Similarly, the additional cost of the suggested counteroffer is the difference between the current cost and the cost of the suggested counteroffer. This calculation should be entered in cell D11.

The cost of the health and dental plans (B13) is merely the sum of the columns from the database that contain the individual expenses of the health plan and the dental plan. Thus, the entry in cell B13 is the addition of the following two statistical functions @SUM:

@SUM(range)+@SUM(range)

Cell C14 is the cost of the full-time counselor under the union's proposal. The HR staff estimates that it can hire a counselor for $30,000 per year plus the approximate 24% cost of benefits.

Cell D15 is the cost of the additional insurance for psychiatric care. Enter the sum of cells R51..R82. The maximum cost of the contracted counseling under the counteroffer is the product of the count of the number of employees in this bargaining unit, the $50 per hour charge, and the 16 weeks maximum of weekly one-hour counseling sessions. Using the statistical function @COUNT, count the number of employees in the database; then multiply the count by the per hour charge and the maximum number of allowable hours of counseling per employee.

You may now sum the additional costs of the union's proposal and the suggested counteroffer. These formulas should be entered in cells C18 and

D18, respectively.

Saving Your Worksheets

Save your work onto the Working Diskette by using the appropriate Lotus 1-2-3 File commands. (For assistance in using the File commands, consult Chapter 2.

Printing the Results

Before beginning to print the results, check to see that you have edited cell A3 and typed your name after the word **Name:**. Print the output screen by establishing a range of cells, A1..D39. (You may seek assistance in printing the results by consulting the section on Lotus 1-2-3 Print Commands in Chapter 2.)

Analyzing the Results

You may now evaluate the union's proposal and the counteroffer made by one of the members of the hospital management's negotiating team. In the space provided, answer the questions at the end of this chapter. Then tear out that page, attach it to the printed results, and turn both in to your instructor.

Endnotes

1. James F. Scearce and Lucretia Dewey Tanner, "Health Care Bargaining: The FMCS Experience," Labor Law Journal, 27 (July, 1976), 387-398.
2. George W. Bohlander and Kevin C. O'Neill, "Health Care Bargaining Unit Determination: Congressional Intent and National Labor Relations Board Decisions," Labor Studies Journal, 5 (Spring, 1980), 25-41.

Questions

1. How does the union's proposal differ from the counteroffer?

2. On what can you base your argument for the union's accepting the counteroffer concerning vacation? (Hint: Review total costs of both the union's proposal and the counteroffer and carefully compare the columns in the index table.)

3. On what basis can you argue for accepting the counteroffer of psychiatric care and hourly counseling? What are the advantages to the employee and the hospital?

4. Of what value is a HR information system during the collective bargaining process?

CHAPTER 14
DISCIPLINARY ACTION: MONITORING THE GRIEVANCE SYSTEM

Lotus 1-2-3 applications in this chapter:

Command Menus
    FILE
    PRINT
    COPY
    DATA QUERY
    DATA SORT

Chapter Outline

Background of the Exercise
Retrieving GRIEVE
Output Screen
Input Screen
Analysis
Saving Your Worksheets
Printing the Results
Analyzing the Results

Whether unionized or nonunionized, many organizations have found that formal grievance procedures offer a number of advantages. Among the advantages is the message communicated by such formal grievance procedures. That message is one of concern for the employees' feelings of having been wronged. Although most organizations strive to treat their employees fairly and within the law, there are occasions when employees _feel_ that they have not been treated fairly and occasions when they have truly been treated unfairly.

The availability of a grievance system leads employees to perceive that there is a legitimate internal channel of communication for feelings of having been wronged. Without this internal channel of communication, employees' grievances will be expressed in other ways. Some of those ways include reduced morale and job satisfaction within the workplace. They may also include intentional sabotage and poor treatment of customers. Few organizations can afford any of these counterproductive behaviors. Therefore, many nonunionized organizations have turned to grievance machinery that is somewhat similar to the grievance procedures established in union contracts.

Background of the Exercise

At Metro Hospital there are informal and formal procedures for grievances. The informal procedure consists of going to one's supervisor and informally discussing the grievance. The staff of the HR Department recognizes that grievances are most easily settled at the informal level between supervisor and employee. As grievances move through formal procedures, they generally take on a character which limits the expression of the emotion that accompanied the original grievance. This limitation means that a portion of the grievance may remain unresolved in the formal system. Therefore, the HR staff has encouraged supervisors to be willing to discuss and negotiate a resolution to an employee's informal expression of unfair treatment.

Of course, because of their very nature some grievances (e.g., sexual harassment by a supervisor or error on a supervisor's part) do not lend themselves to easy informal resolution at the supervisory level. Thus, a formal grievance system is necessary. The staff of the HR Department has expressed strong confidence in its formal procedure in order to build its credibility among employees. This procedure consists of (1) a formal, written appeal to the supervisor, (2) a written appeal to the supervisor's manager, (3) a written appeal to the Director of Human Resources, and (4) a written appeal to the Director of the Hospital.

The HR staff maintains a record within its HR Database of each formal grievance based on its jurisdiction and disposition. The **jurisdiction** is the area or topic of the grievance. Among the potential jurisdictions of grievances are the following: job duties (inappropriate or unfair assignment of tasks), environment (some aspect of the environment which makes it unpleasant or difficult in which to work), safety, racial discrimination, discrimination based on religion, sex discrimination, sexual harassment, age discrimination, discrimination based on national origin, discrimination based on handicap, etc.

The **disposition** of the grievance refers to the final action taken as a result of its having been filed and adjudicated. Dispositions include referring the grievance back to the supervisor for his/her resolution, internal referral of the grievance to another department for its resolution, taking no action, resolving the grievance with no further action from the employee, and having the grievance filed with an outside agency such as the Equal Employment Opportunity Commission.

At the close of each fiscal year, Metro Hospital's HR staff reviews the jurisdiction and disposition of its grievances for the year. The purpose of this review is to (1) identify any problem departments within the hospital, (2) identify any problem areas (themes or concerns of employees), and (3) evaluate the effectiveness of the formal procedure.

Retrieving GRIEVE

Retrieve the file called GRIEVE from your HR Data Diskette. Then replace the HR Data Diskette with the Working Diskette.

Output Screen

The output screen includes cells A1..K24 (see Exhibit 14-1). This area contains space for you to write the information that you will need about each employee who has filed a formal grievance. There is also space for you to establish the criterion upon which the database inquiries are made.

Input Screen

In the area A27..K130 is a slice of the HR Database containing the records of nonmanagerial employees at Metro Hospital. Selected fields of information about these employees include: Name (of the employee), Date of Hire, Date of Birth, Race, Sex, Job Title, Department, Exempt (status), Grievance ("Y" for Yes, if filed), Jurisdiction, and Disposition.

Analysis

To complete the required analysis, you will need to extract information about the employees who have filed grievances. Your first step is to type the word Criterion in cell A7. In the two cells below it, type the appropriate field name for a search for those who have filed a grievance. Below the field name, type the criterion or label that you will use to match against the cases in the database. To determine which field name and which label to use in establishing the criterion, review the field names given earlier in this chapter. You may also wish to review the database in the worksheet area, A27..K130.

While in the Ready mode, also enter the field names that you will need to identify the output area when "creating a database." Copy the field names from the database input screen at A30..K30 and enter them in row 12, beginning with cell A12.

You are now ready to create the database using the Lotus 1-2-3 database command menu. Be sure to include the field names of the HR Database when you establish the input area and the output area. The input area is A30..K130, and the output area should be A12..K24.

As you review the employee records, you may find that your analyses can be facilitated by sorting the extracted records based on the jurisdiction of the grievances or the department. In fact, you may wish to complete both sorts independently and review the data before completing the second sort. (For assistance in sorting the extracted records, consult the subsection on the Lotus 1-2-3 Sort Command of the Data Management section in Chapter 2.)

Exhibit 14-1

GRIEVE
Disciplinary Action: Monitoring The Grievance System
Name:

OUTPUT

Saving Your Worksheets

Save your work onto the Working Diskette by using the appropriate Lotus 1-2-3 File commands. (For assistance in using the File commands, consult Chapter 2.)

Printing the Results

Before beginning to print the results, check to see that you have edited cell A3 and typed your name after the word **Name:**. Since these data will cover more than one standard page of output, you will need to follow these steps. First, establish a print range of B1..K24. With the Lotus 1-2-3 Print command menu at the top of the screen, type OBC (OPTIONS BORDER COLUMNS). At the following Lotus 1-2-3 prompt:

Enter Border Columns:

type A1 for column A which contains the names of the employees who have filed grievances. Press the Enter key to store the border column. To leave this Options submenu, type Q (QUIT) and continue by printing the results. (You may seek assistance in printing the results by consulting the section on Lotus 1-2-3 Print Commands in Chapter 2.)

Analyzing the Results

You may now review the formal grievance system in order to (1) identify any problem departments within the hospital, (2) identify any problem areas (themes or concerns of employees), and (3) evaluate the effectiveness of the formal procedure. In the space provided, answer the questions at the end of this chapter. Then tear out that page, attach it to the printed results, and turn both in to your instructor.

Questions

1. Are there any departments which have an abnormally large number of grievances relative to the other departments?

2. Are there any common problem themes among the grievances?

3. How effective is Metro's formal grievance procedure?

4. What recommendations, if any, will you make to the HR staff concerning its grievance procedure or other aspects of managing grievances?

CHAPTER 15
MANAGING EMPLOYEE COMPENSATION

Lotus 1-2-3 applications in this chapter:

Command Menus
   FILE
   PRINT
   COPY
Mathematical Operations
   Addition
   Subtraction
   Multiplication
   Division
Statistical Functions
   @SUM
   @STD
   @MAX
   @MIN

Chapter Outline

Employee compensation represents a large expense for any organization. For this reason alone, it is important for an organization to manage carefully its compensation system. Large companies, as well as increasing numbers of smaller companies, are systematically designing their compensation systems to assure that they can manage this costly aspect of their budgets.

There are other important reasons for paying close attention to salaries and the design of the compensation system. Salaries play a critical role in raising productivity levels of employees. Many organizations tie salaries directly to the productivity levels or performance appraisals of their employees. The more productive employees receive higher salary increases. The intended effect is to reward those who have been productive and to encourage employees who need to improve their productivity by enhancing their motivational level.[1] We know that employees compare their salaries with one another. Those who feel that they have put effort into their work for which they are not being fairly compensated feel a sense of

inequity, and this inequity reduces their motivational levels and subsequent performance.[2]

A final reason for the concern of organizations with wages is their
desire to retain their employees. Organizations must assure themselves
that their wages are comparable to those of competitors in their geographical areas. If an organization's wages fall below the market level,
then employees may leave to obtain jobs with those organizations that are
paying higher wages.

Inflation also sometimes plays a role in employees' perceived market
equity of salaries. As prices in the economy rise, employees apply increasingly powerful pressure on their employers to give them wage increases that will maintain their current buying power. Organizations have
found themselves faced with a need to offer cost-of-living adjustments
(COLAs) as a response to that pressure from their employees.

Pressure also comes from other organizations that offer COLAs; a
company may find its employees with relatively lower salaries if it does
not offer COLAs. To avoid losing its employees, the company feels com-
pelled to also offer a COLA. Because many economists have argued that
there are increasing inflationary pressures in the economy, it will be important for an organization to have the capability to analyze with ease
the impact of a COLA.

Background of the Exercise

Given modest inflation over the past few years, Metro Hospital has
not been faced with great pressure to increase its overall wages with a
COLA. The last across-the-board adjustment in its compensation system was
made two years ago. Data from the Business Bureau of the local state university pegged inflation for this year at 4.8 percent in the state. From
these same data, there were projections of a 5.6 percent inflation rate
for the next year.

Despite the lack of visible internal pressure for a COLA, Metro is
concerned about the possible need to raise its overall compensation pack-
age for its employees. Since Metro contributes information about its
salaries to a statewide wage survey, it receives information about the
median, mean, and range of salaries in various health-care-related job
categories. The most recent survey provided data that led some of the HR
staff to conclude that Metro was paying wages that were just at the median
level for the state. Thus, its salaries may not be enough to retain the
very best employees. The HR staff intends to calculate the wage costs associated with two possible across-the-board increases in salaries.

In addition to its concern with the overall level of wages, the HR
staff has been concerned with the degree to which Metro's wages for various jobs remain in line with the demands or worth of those jobs. At Metro
Hospital the compensation system is based on a series of job grades. Each
job grade includes a range of points from a point-factor method of job

analysis used by the HR staff. Jobs are assigned to a specific grade based on the number of points allocated through a structured job analysis using the point-factor method. Among the 11 factors included in the job analysis were education, complexity of decision making, effect of errors, etc.

The HR staff wants to make sure that the grade and salary steps have been set up reasonably to value the worth of a given job. The staff knows that undervaluing a job may result in perceived inequity, lower motivation, and turnover. If the pay grade system has been well designed and maintained, there should be a strong association or high correlation between the midpoints of the point distribution and the midpoints of the grades.

Retrieving WAGES

To evaluate the impact of the proposed COLAs and evaluate the association between wages and job grades, retrieve the file called WAGES from the HR Data Diskette. Then replace the HR Data diskette with your Working Diskette.

Output Screen

The output screen includes cells A1..D47 and consists of two types of analyses (see Exhibit 15-1). The first analysis deals with the impact of two alternative COLAs; the second analysis deals with the association between the points of a given grade and the wages associated with the grade.

Two-Part Input Screen

There are two parts of the input screen. The first part is a slice of the HR Database that includes cells A52..J175. This screen contains the following fields: Name, Race, Sex, Date of Hire, Job Title, Department, Factor Points (points assigned to a job by means of the point factor method of job analysis), Salary Grade, Salary Step, and Annual Salary.

The second part of the input screen is located in cells L53..Y74 (see Exhibit 15-2) and is the index table of information about the grades and steps of the compensation system. Go to L53 to review this index table, which contains data for 13 salary grades. Beneath each grade (e.g., G1 for Grade 1) is information about the factor points that are associated with that grade. Grade 1 (G1) covers those jobs that have been rated between 231 and 275 factor points.

Also in each of the Grade columns are the 12 salary steps for each grade. Employees whose jobs are classified in Grade 1 start at a salary of $7,176. This salary is the base for the entire table. You will observe that all other salaries in this table are multiples of this number. For example, the salary for Step 2 in Grade 1 is $7,463--$7,176 multiplied by an index factor of 1.04. You will also observe that the Step 1 salary of each grade is derived from the previous grade's Step 5 salary.

Exhibit 15-1

WAGES
Managing Employee Compensation
Name:

OUTPUT SCREEN

COLA ANALYSIS

TOTAL COST WAGES =	$0
INDEX FACTOR(1) =	0
NEW COST(1) =	$0
ADDITION (1) =	$0
INDEX FACTOR (2)	0
NEW COST(2) =	$0
ADDITION (2) =	$0

PAY GRADE ANALYSIS

GRADES	POINTS MIDPOINT	WAGES MIDPOINT	CROSS PRODUCT
GRADE 1	0	$0	0
GRADE 2	0	$0	0
GRADE 3	0	$0	0
GRADE 4	0	$0	0
GRADE 5	0	$0	0
GRADE 6	0	$0	0
GRADE 7	0	$0	0
GRADE 8	0	$0	0
GRADE 9	0	$0	0
GRADE 10	0	$0	0
GRADE 11	0	$0	0
GRADE 12	0	$0	0
GRADE 13	0	$0	0

Correlation:

Mean of Points	0.00
Mean of Wages	$0
Standard Dev. - Points	0.00
Standard Dev. - Wages	$0
Sum of Cross Products	0
Count of Grades (N)	13
Correlation Coefficient	0.00

Exhibit 15-2

PAY GRADES

GRADE	G1	G2	G3	G4	G5	G6	G7	G8	G9	G10	G11	G12	G13
MIN POINTS	231	276	301	326	351	401	501	576	651	726	801	851	901
MAX POINTS	275	300	325	350	400	500	575	650	725	800	850	900	950
MID POINT	0	0	0	0	0	0	0	0	0	0	0	0	0
STEPS													
1	7176	8395	9821	11489	13441	15723	18394	21519	25174	29450	34452	40304	47150
2	7463	8731	10214	11949	13978	16352	19130	22379	26181	30628	35830	41916	49036
3	7762	9080	10622	12427	14537	17007	19895	23275	27228	31853	37263	43593	50998
4	8072	9443	11047	12924	15119	17687	20691	24206	28317	33127	38754	45337	53037
5	8395	9821	11489	13441	15723	18394	21519	25174	29450	34452	40304	47150	55159
6	8731	10214	11949	13978	16352	19130	22379	26181	30628	35830	41916	49036	57365
7	9080	10622	12427	14537	17007	19895	23275	27228	31853	37263	43593	50998	59660
8	9443	11047	12924	15119	17687	20691	24206	28317	33127	38754	45337	53037	62046
9	9821	11489	13441	15723	18394	21519	25174	29450	34452	40304	47150	55159	64528
10	10214	11949	13978	16352	19130	22379	26181	30628	35830	41916	49036	57365	67109
11	10622	12427	14537	17007	19895	23275	27228	31853	37263	43593	50998	59660	69794
12	11047	12924	15119	17687	20691	24206	28317	33127	38754	45337	53037	62046	72585
MIDPOINT	0	0	0	0	0	0	0	0	0	0	0	0	0

Analysis

COLA Analysis. The purpose of this analysis is to calculate the costs of two possible COLAs: one at 3% and the other at 5.75%.

Return to the output screen at cell A1. Begin by calculating the Total Cost Wages at cell B10. This is done by summing the column of data which begins at cell J55 beneath the column labeled Annual Salary. Enter the appropriate statistical function for summing this column of data in cell B10.

Metro Hospital is considering a 3% COLA for its employees. Thus, Index Factor (1) in row 12 is 1.03. The 3% raise is written as an index factor so that the total cost of wages that was calculated in cell B10 can be easily multiplied to provide the total cost of the new wages including the 3% increase. Enter the index factor for the 3% increase in cell B12.

To calculate New Cost (1), it is necessary to multiply the Total Cost Wages by the Index Factor (1). Enter a formula for this calculation in B13. Calculate Addition (1) to the cost of wages by subtracting Total Cost Wages from New Cost (1).

Metro Hospital is also considering a 5.75% COLA. Make the required entries in cells B16, B17, and B18 to provide data similar to that associated with the 3% increase.

Pay Grade Analysis. Metro Hospital is concerned about the degree to which its wages correspond to the worth of its jobs. This analysis requires that you calculate a correlation coefficient for two sets of data: (1) the midpoints of the point-factor distribution, and (2) the midpoints of the salary levels by grade.

In cells L53 through Y74 are data for the 13 grades (G1 through G13). In each column, the minimum points and the maximum points for the grade are indicated. For example, the minimum for G1 (Grade 1) is in cell M57, and the maximum for G2 is in N58. Cells M59..Y59 contain zeros where you must enter a formula for calculating the midpoints. To calculate the midpoint, subtract the minimum points from the maximum; divide the result by two; and add the remainder to the minimum. Here is the general form of this formula:

$$\textbf{((Maximum-Minimum)/2)+Minimum}$$

You may use a cell address for the maximum and minimum, or you may use the Lotus 1-2-3 statistical functions @MAX and @MIN.

Once you have written this formula into cell M59, copy it to N59..Y59. The midpoints are automatically copied to the output screen B25..B37.

The pay grade analysis also requires the midpoints of the salary ranges within each grade. Cells M74..Y74 contain zeros where the required formulas must be entered for calculating these midpoints. Using salary minima and maxima, follow the same general formula that you used in calculating the midpoints for the factor points. Also copy this formula from M74 to N74..Y74. The salary midpoints are automatically copied to the output screen C25..C37.

After completing the calculations for the midpoints of factor points and salary ranges, return to the output screen at cell A21, where you will see the results of the midpoint calculations. At A40..B47 are the various elements required for calculating a correlation coefficient.

Begin by calculating a mean (average) of the two distributions of midpoints. In cell B41, use the Lotus 1-2-3 statistical function @AVG to calculate the mean of the data at B25..B37. In B42, use the same statistical function for calculating the mean of the distribution of salary midpoints.

The standard deviation is a measure of the dispersion or spread of the data. It is calculated with the following Lotus 1-2-3 statistical function:

@STD(cellx..celly)

Cell B43 requires a standard deviation for the midpoints of the factor-point distribution--the data in cells B25..B37. Cell B44 requires a standard deviation for the midpoints of the wage ranges--the data in cells C25..C37.

The sum of the cross products is requested in cell B45. This calculation is a bit unusual; however, it is necessary for the formula that you will use to calculate the correlation coefficient. To calculate the sum of the cross products, go to cell D25 and enter the formula for the product of the Points Midpoint (B25) and the Wages Midpoint (C25). Now copy this formula to cells D26..D37. Then return to cell B45 and enter the Lotus 1-2-3 statistical function for summing the cross products in cells D25..D37. You now have the sum of the cross products.

As the term suggests, correlation is the interrelationship between sets of data. Here it is the relationship between the factor points for each grade and the wages associated with each grade. A zero correlation says that there is no relationship between the two sets of data, and a correlation of 1.0 says that there is a perfect relationship. If you are interested in the technical characteristics of a correlation coefficient, you may wish to consult a basic textbook on statistics.

From the calculations you have just completed, you can see that a correlation coefficient is composed of several important elements: the means of the sets of data, their cross products, their standard deviations, and the number of entries--the N in cell B46. Here is a formula for the correlation coefficient:

$$((\text{sum of cross products}/N)-(\text{Mean}_1*\text{Mean}_2))/(\text{STD}_1*\text{STD}_2)$$

This formula states that a correlation is the mean of the sum of the cross products minus the product of the two means, all of which is divided by the product of the standard deviations. For cell B47, it will be written as:

$$((+B45/B46)-(B41*B42))/(B43*B44)$$

Saving Your Worksheets

Save your work onto the Working Diskette by using the appropriate Lotus 1-2-3 File commands. (For assistance in using the File commands, consult Chapter 2.)

Printing the Results

Before beginning to print the results, check to see that you have edited cell A3 and typed your name after the word **Name:**. Print the output screen by establishing a range of cells A1..D47. (You may seek assistance in printing the results by consulting the section on Lotus 1-2-3 Print Commands in Chapter 2.)

Analyzing the Results

You may now evaluate the COLAs and the association between the points in the point-factor system of job evaluation and the wages associated with each grade of the system. In the space provided, answer the questions at the end of this chapter. Then tear out that page, attach it to the printed results, and turn both in to your instructor.

Endnotes

1. For a discussion of the role of rewards on performance, see Fred Luthans and Robert Kreitner, Organizational Behavior Modification and Beyond: An Operant and Social Learning Approach (Glenview, IL: Scott, Foresman, 1985).

2. J. Stacy Adams is generally credited for explaining the effect of perceived equity. See J. Stacy Adams, "Toward an Understanding of Inequity," Journal of Abnormal and Social Psychology, 67 (1963), 422-436.

Questions

1. What are the impacts of the two COLAs?

2. Evaluate the elements of the compensation system about which you are aware.

   a. How close is the association between points and salaries?

   b. What is a better alternative way to assess the association?

3. How does a database (such as the one here) aid you in changing the
    salaries if a COLA is offered?

CHAPTER 16
SAFETY AND HEALTH

Lotus 1-2-3 applications in this chapter:

Command Menus
   FILE
   PRINT
   COPY
   DATA QUERY
   DATA SORT
Mathematical Operations
   Multiplication
   Division
Statistical Functions
   @COUNT
   @SUM
Date and Time Functions
   @DATE*

Chapter Outline

Background of the Exercise
Retrieving SAFETY
Output Screen
Input Screen
Analysis
   Completing OSHA Form No. 200
   Calculating the Incidence Rate
Saving Your Worksheets
Printing the Results
Analyzing the Results

Interest in large-scale improvements in the health and safety of America's work force stretches back at least to the middle of the nineteenth century. In 1869, Pennsylvania passed the first state law for coal mine inspections. In 1908, the nation's first workers' compensation law was passed; it covered only federal employees. A series of developments in state and federal government as well as in various industries, such as mining and steel, led to increasingly safer conditions for the country's labor force. With these improvements came the passage of the Occupational Safety and Health Act in 1970 and the creation of the National Institute for Occupational Safety and Health (NIOSH) in 1971. Partly as a result of these changes, the overall work-related accident rate per 100 persons per year is now 7.1, and the rate in the health-services industry is 3.4.[1]

---

*Indicates a first-time use of this Lotus 1-2-3 application in this book.

Although the Occupational Safety and Health Act has created numerous requirements for safety in industry, it is clear that safety is ultimately the responsibility of the individual organization. An organization must (1) provide leadership in dealing with the health and safety of its employees, (2) establish safe and healthful working conditions, and (3) encourage safe work practices by its employees.[2] No restriction nor regulation of the state or local government will substitute for these three essential elements of an organization's health and safety program.

Background of the Exercise

Metro Hospital's senior management has maintained an active health and safety program for its employees. It has used the traditional methods of assuring the safety and health of its employees, including providing protective gear to employees, assuring that machinery is safe, insisting on strict procedures for handling dangerous and infectious materials, and communicating frequently about rules and procedures associated with employee health and safety. Metro has also adopted a program of employee fitness which encourages employee participation in daily exercise in order to improve cardiovascular functions, strengthen the body, and reduce the total amount of fat in body weight.

In addition to such efforts, Metro Hospital complies with the requirements of the Occupational Safety and Health Act, including the reporting requirements. Like other companies. it completes and posts the summary information from OSHA Form No. 200. Since Metro has a HR Database, it has opted to summarize its accident and injury report information by establishing the required elements from OSHA Form No. 200 within its database. Metro also computes an incidence rate for its yearly total of accidents and injuries. It uses this rate to evaluate its efforts to maintain a safe and healthy work environment for its employees.

Metro's HR staff is preparing its annual OSHA Form 200 report. To do this, the staff is reviewing the various required elements of Form 200. Each element, with its Form No. 200 alphanumeric column designation and label, is listed below. Accompanying the OSHA labels are the field names (in parentheses) that the staff uses in its HR Database:

Column	Labels and Field Names
Column A	Case or file Number (CASE)
Column B	Date of injury or onset of illness (DATE)
Column C	Employee's name (NAME)
Column D	Occupation (JOB TITLE)
Column E	Department (DEPARTMENT)
Column F	Description of injury or illness (DESCRIPTION)
Column 1	Date of death from injury (FATALITY)

Column	Labels and Field Names

Column 2   Enter a check if injury results in days away from work or days of restricted activity or both (RESTRICTION)

Column 3   Enter a check if injury involves days away from work (ABSENCE)

Column 4   Enter number of days away from work (DAYS)

Column 5   Enter number of days of restricted work activity (ACTIVITY)

Column 6   Enter a check if the injury led neither to death nor days away from work nor restricted work activity (NO LOSS)

Column 7   Indicate the type of illness (TYPE)

      A   Occupational skin diseases (e.g., dermatitis)

      B   Dust diseases of the lungs (e.g., asbestosis)

      C   Respiratory conditions due to toxic agents (e.g., rhinitis)

      D   Poisoning via the systemic effect of toxic materials (e.g., lead poisoning)

      E   Disorders due to physical agents other than toxic materials (e.g., heat stroke)

      F   Disorders associated with repeated trauma (e.g., noise-induced hearing loss)

      G   All other occupational illnesses (e.g., hepatitis)

Column 8   Date of death from illness (DEATH)

Column 9   Enter a check if illness results in days away from work or days of restricted activity or both (LIMITATION)

Column 10   Enter a check if illness involves days away from work (TIME)

Column 11   Enter number of days away from work (AWAY)

Column 12   Enter number of days of restricted work activity (RESTRICTED)

Column 13   Enter a check if the illness led neither to death nor days away from work nor restricted work activity (W/O LOSS)

Your tasks are to (1) complete OSHA Form No. 200 for the HR staff, and (2) calculate an incidence rate of injuries and illnesses.

Retrieving SAFETY

To accomplish your tasks, retrieve the file called SAFETY from your HR Data Diskette. Then replace the HR Data Diskette with your Working Diskette.

Output Screen

The output screen is located in cells A1..S29 (see Exhibit 16-1a, 16-1b, and 16-1c). It includes the criterion A9..A10 upon which the database will be searched for employees who have had a reportable injury or illness. For Metro's database, this criterion is based on the field which contains the date of the injury or illness and a seemingly complicated formula that appears as a zero in cell A10. You can view the following formula at the top of the screen by moving the cursor to A10:

$$+U36<(@DATE(88,1,1))\#AND\#U37>(@DATE(86,12,31))$$

This formula results in a search for all accident dates that occurred between the end of 1986 and the beginning of 1988--i.e., the year 1987. While the formula is complicated, it is typical of formulas that are used as database criteria in Lotus 1-2-3. Such formulas use the cell address of the cell immediately below the field name in the database. Note that the employee whose record is stored on row 37 has not had a reportable injury or illness; therefore, the formula leads to a zero being written in cell A10.

The output screen also contains the field names used in the HR Database for storing the required information for each of the columns of OSHA Form No. 200. The field names included for the report are: Case, Date, Name, Job Title, Department, Injury/Illness Description, Date of Fatality, Work Restriction, Work Absence, Absence Days, Restricted Activity, Injury No Loss, Illness Type, Illness Death, Illness Limitation, Absence Time, Days Away, Days Restricted, and Illness W/O Loss.

The final part of the output screen contains the necessary elements for calculating the incidence rate of accidents and injuries.

Input Screen

The input screen is located in cells C33..U156. It is the slice of the database included in these analyses along with the various fields associated with accident reporting. Three standard fields from the HR Database are included in this slice of the database: Name, Job Title, and Department. The remaining additional field names, associated with accident reporting, are the same as those noted previously in this chapter.

Exhibit 16-1a

SAFETY
Safety and Health
Name:

OUTPUT

Criterion

DATE
0

OSHA No. 200

A	B	C	D	E
CASE	DATE	NAME	JOB TITLE	DEPARTMENT

TOTAL

Incidence Rate	
Number of injuries and illnesses	0
Number of employees	0
Number hours worked	0
Rate	0.00

Exhibit 16-1b

F INJURY/ILLNESS DESCRIPTION	1 DATE OF FATALITY	2 WORK RESTRICTION	3 WORK ABSENCE	4 ABSENCE DAYS	5 RESTRICTED ACTIVITY	6 INJURY NO LOSS	7 ILLNESS TYPE	8 ILLNESS DEATH	9 ILLNESS LIMITATION
	0	0	0	0	0	0	0	0	0

Exhibit 16-1c

13 DAYS ILLNESS RESTRICTED W/O LOSS

12 DAYS RESTRICTED

11 DAYS AWAY

10 ABSENCE TIME

Analysis

The first step in the analysis is to update the database by entering information for an accident which occurred to Stephen Herzel, a security officer. First, find the name of this security officer in the database. Mr. Herzel was killed on November 11, 1987, in an automobile accident while he was on duty for the hospital. Column F of OSHA Form No. 200 requires a description of the injury or illness. This information is stored beneath the label DESCRIPTION within the HR Database. Now find this column within the database and describe the accident "killed in auto accident" on row 84 where Herzel's employee record is located.

Next, find the Lotus 1-2-3 column for reporting the date of the fatality within the database. Then enter the date of the accident on row 84, using the Lotus 1-2-3 statistical function @DATE. This statistical function takes the following general form:

@DATE(two digit year, month number, day of month)

If you do not know on which worksheet column to enter the date, return to the Background of the Exercise in this chapter and review the required entries in OSHA Form No. 200 along with the labels used in the HR Database for each required entry. Then scan row 35, which contains the database labels, to find the correct column for the row 84 entry.

A consecutive case number of 37 and the date of the report should be typed in the appropriate columns. In this case, the date of the report is the same as the date of the accident. Again, if you need help in finding the correct column to enter the case number and the date of the report, review the required entries for OSHA Form 200 which were listed earlier in this chapter. Then review row 35 for the label which is used in the HR Database for this entry. Return to cell A1 (Home).

Completing OSHA Form No. 200. The next steps in the analysis lead to building Form No. 200. To build this form from the HR Database, "create a database" with the Lotus 1-2-3 database command menu. The input area should include all of the records as well as the single row of field names at the top of the records. The output area is A16..S21. The criterion, which was identified earlier in this chapter, is A9..A10.

After extracting the employee records for which there was an injury or illness report during the reporting period, review them. You will note that the order is not according to case number. Instead, the order is alphabetical, as are the records in the database. For the OSHA No. 200 report, you will want to list the accidents in the order of their case numbers; therefore, sort the data by case number. (For assistance in sorting records, consult the subsection on Sorting Records under the section on Data Management in Chapter 2.)

OSHA Form No. 200 also requires that the totals be posted for the numbered columns. Therefore, use the statistical function @COUNT to count the entries in columns 1, 2, 3, 6, 7, 8, 9, 10, and 13 of Form No. 200 (on the Lotus 1-2-3 worksheet, these Form No. 200 columns are columns G, H, I, L, M, N, O, P, and S). Use the statistical function @SUM to add the entries in Form No. 200 columns 4, 5, 11, and 12 (worksheet columns J, K, Q, and R).

Calculating the Incidence Rate. The worksheet area for calculating the accident incidence rate is A25..D29. To complete this area, several calculations are required. First, count the number of injuries and illnesses by using the Lotus 1-2-3 statistical function @COUNT in D26. Use the same statistical function @COUNT to count the number of employees in this slice of the database. (For assistance in using these statistical functions, consult the section on Statistical Functions in Chapter 2.)

Second, in cell D28 calculate the number of hours worked in the year. Assume that each of the employees you counted for cell D27 worked 52 weeks for 40 hours per week. Thus, multiply the number in cell D27 by 52 and 40. Be sure to use the worksheet address of D27 in the calculation rather than the number on the screen.

Finally, calculate the incidence rate with the following formula:

(Number of injuries and illnesses * 200,000) / Employee hours worked)

The number 200,000 is used as a standard, and it represents 100 employees working for 52 weeks at 40 hours per week. In cell D29, enter a Lotus 1-2-3 formula for calculating the incidence rate.

Saving Your Worksheets

Save your work onto the Working Diskette by using the appropriate Lotus 1-2-3 File commands. (For assistance in using the File commands, consult Chapter 2.)

Printing the Results

Before beginning to print the results, check to see that you have edited cell A3 and typed your name after the word **Name:**. Print the output screen by establishing a range of cells A1..S29. Since this output screen is unusually wide, you may wish to use "condensed" printing rather than the usual 10 or 12 characters per inch. If you do this, you will need some assistance in choosing and entering the proper setup character as well as in changing the right margin. (You may seek assistance in printing the results by consulting the section on Lotus 1-2-3 Print Commands in Chapter 2; however, the proper setup character depends on the particular printer you are using and this situation is not discussed in Chapter 2 of this book. You will need to consult your instructor, your laboratory instructor, or the manual which accompanies your printer for the correct setup codes for your printer.)

Analyzing the Results

    You may now evaluate OSHA Form No. 200 and the incidence rate at
Metro Hospital. In the space provided, answer the questions at the end of
this chapter.   Then tear out that page, attach it to the printed results,
and turn both in to your instructor.

Endnotes

    1. Data from the Bureau of Labor Statistics are reported in National
Safety Council, Accident Facts: 1987 Edition (Chicago: National Safety
Council, 1987), p. 38.
    2. Thomas J. Anton, Occupational Safety and Health Management (New
York: McGraw-Hill Book Company, 1979).

Questions

1. How does a HR information system aid you in completing a governmental form such as OSHA No. 200?

2. Does Metro Hospital have a particular type of safety or health hazard that it should address? If yes, what is it and why have you selected this hazard? If no, why not?

3. Compare the incidence rate at Metro Hospital with the industry rate. What comments or recommendations can you make as a result of this comparison?

CHAPTER 17
AUDITING THE HUMAN RESOURCES MANAGEMENT PROGRAM

Lotus 1-2-3 applications in this chapter:

Command Menus
   FILE
   PRINT
   COPY
Mathematical Operations
   Multiplication
   Division
Statistical Functions
   @COUNT
Database Statistical Functions
   @DSUM*
   @DCOUNT

Chapter Outline

Background of the Exercise
Retrieving AUDIT
Output Screen
Input Screen
Analysis
Saving Your Worksheets
Printing the Results
Analyzing the Results

One of the major advantages of a HR database is the ease with which various aspects of the HR system may be audited. The availability of data and the ability to manipulate the data easily are resulting in a substantial increase in the use of HR audits by professionals within the field.

Such audits are appropriate for a variety of reasons. They provide important information about an organization so that the management of the HR function can be improved. They also offer a means to evaluate the cost effectiveness of various managerial strategies that an organization adopts. For example, changes in the appraisal system can be evaluated through attitude surveys; or audits of turnover and absenteeism may be used to highlight potential sources of organizational problems.

---

*Indicates a first-time use of this Lotus 1-2-3 application in this book.

Background of the Exercise

The HR staff of Metro Hospital has decided to review its absenteeism rates with the intention of highlighting problem areas within the organization as well as evaluating the rates of absenteeism within the hospital. The staff of the HR Department has generally believed that its absenteeism rate is reasonable. It has learned that the mean or average number of days off the job is 3.1 for all workers in all industries.[1] Thus, the nation-wide absenteeism rate is about 3.5, based on the standard formula for calculating absenteeism rates.[2]

Through its HR Database, the staff can easily analyze the rate in various specific departments. The staff has decided to evaluate the overall absenteeism rate as well as the rates for the following selected departments: Data Processing, OBGYN, Accounting, Housekeeping, Radiology, and Social Services. This cross section of departments should provide insight into absenteeism in a variety of areas within the hospital.

The mere rate of absenteeism often fails to provide the entire story about absenteeism. Therefore, the staff made the decision to calculate the cost of absenteeism based on the wages of those who have been absent. The staff has used an across-the-board percentage of salary in order to estimate the cost of benefits as well. Finally, the staff wants to compare the rate of absenteeism and the cost of absenteeism for a given department with the overall rate and costs.

Retrieving AUDIT

To assist the staff in these analyses, retrieve the file called AUDIT from your HR Data Diskette. Then replace the HR Data Diskette with your Working Diskette.

Output Screen

The output screen is found in cells A1..B97 (see Exhibits 17-1a and 17-1b). The data for the overall absenteeism rate includes hours lost due to absence, days lost, the number of employees in this slice of the database, the number of workdays in the period under analysis, the absenteeism rate, the total cost of wages lost due to absenteeism, the cost of benefits paid for lost work, and the total cost.

The output screen also includes data for the departments in which the staff is particularly interested. For each of these departments, data required for the overall analysis will be needed, as well as data for the percentage of the total employees represented by this department and the percentage of the total cost of absenteeism represented by this department.

Exhibit 17-1a

AUDIT
Auditing the Human Resources Management Program
Name:

OUTPUT

Absenteeism Rate

Overall
Hours Lost   0
Days Lost   0
N of Employees   0
Workdays   0
Rate   0.00%
Cost of Wages $0
Cost of Benefits $0
Total Cost $0

DEPARTMENT
DATA PROCESSING
Hours Lost   0
Days Lost   0
N of Employees   0
Workdays   0
Rate   0.00%
Cost of Wages $0
Cost of Benefits $0
Total Cost $0
% of Total Employees   0.00%
% Absenteeism Cost   0.00%

DEPARTMENT
OBGYN
Hours Lost   0
Days Lost   0
N of Employees   0
Workdays   0
Rate   0.00%
Cost of Wages $0
Cost of Benefits $0
Total Cost $0
% of Total Employees   0.00%
% Absenteeism Cost   0.00%

DEPARTMENT
ACCOUNTING
Hours Lost   0
Days Lost   0
N of Employees   0
Workdays   0
Rate   0.00%
Cost of Wages $0
Cost of Benefits $0
Total Cost $0
% of Total Employees   0.00%
% Absenteeism Cost   0.00%

Exhibit 17-1b

DEPARTMENT
HOUSEKEEPING

Hours Lost	0
Days Lost	0
N of Employees	0
Workdays	0
Rate	0.00%
Cost of Wages	$0
Cost of Benefits	$0
Total Cost	$0
% of Total Employees	0.00%
% Absenteeism Cost	0.00%

DEPARTMENT
RADIOLOGY

Hours Lost	0
Days Lost	0
N of Employees	0
Workdays	0
Rate	0.00%
Cost of Wages	$0
Cost of Benefits	$0
Total Cost	$0
% of Total Employees	0.00%
% Absenteeism Cost	0.00%

DEPARTMENT
SOCIAL SERVICES

Hours Lost	0
Days Lost	0
N of Employees	0
Workdays	0
Rate	0.00%
Cost of Wages	$0
Cost of Benefits	$0
Total Cost	$0
% of Total Employees	0.00%
% Absenteeism Cost	0.00%

Input Screen

The input screen is located in cells A101..G224. This slice of the database includes the following fields: Name, Date of Hire, Job Title, Department, Annual Salary, Yearly Absences (number of hours to date for this period), and Absenteeism Cost. The last field, Absenteeism Cost, was added by the HR staff for just this set of analyses, and the values for each employee must be calculated as a part of your analysis.

Analysis

Your first step is to calculate the cost of lost wages due to absenteeism. This calculation should be done in column G, beginning at G104, the first entry below the field name Absenteeism Cost. The formula that you enter in cell G98 should calculate a total cost to date for this employee. Its general form is:

(Annual Wages/(Months*Days Per Month*Hours Per Day))*Yearly Absences

This formula calculates an hourly cost of wages and multiplies the hourly cost by the number of hours of absenteeism which is recorded in column F. Enter the appropriate Lotus 1-2-3 formula in cell G104. In entering the formula, assume that each month contains 22 work days. Then copy the formula to the remaining cells in G105..G224. (For assistance in copying formulas, consult the section on the Lotus 1-2-3 Copy Command in Chapter 2.)

You are now ready to return to the output screen at cell A7. The first entry called for in cell B12 is the sum of hours lost due to absenteeism. To sum the hours lost from the appropriate column of the HR Database, enter the required statistical function in B12. The number of days lost may be calculated by dividing the value in cell B12 by 8 (the number of hours in the workday).

Cell B14 requires the number of employees in this slice of the database. Use the statistical function @COUNT to count the number of employees in this slice of the HR Database.

Assume that the analysis is covering a four-month period for which there are 88 days (4 * 22). Enter the number 88 in cell B15.

The rate of absenteeism[3] is calculated in cell B16. Its general form is:

(Days Lost / (Number of Employees * Number of Workdays))

Lotus 1-2-3 permits the user to format any section of the worksheet as a percentage. Since this has already been done for cell B16 and corresponding cells for the rate for each department, it is unnecessary for you to multiply by 100 in order to obtain a percentage.

In cell B17, enter the cost of wages lost due to absenteeism. To add the individual costs of lost wages in column G below the field name Absenteeism Cost in the database, use the statistical function @SUM. Since the staff is assuming a 24% cost of benefits, in cell B18 enter a formula that multiplies the Cost of Wages by .24.

The final entry for the overall absenteeism analysis is the Total Cost. It is merely the sum of the Cost of Wages and the Cost of Benefits. Add these two entries in cell B19.

The remaining parts of the analysis are similar to what you have just completed, but they are designed for the specific departments. For example, absenteeism data for the Data Processing Department should be calculated in cells A21..B32. Similar calculations are required for OBGYN, Accounting, Housekeeping, Radiology, and Social Services.

Although the calculations for each department are similar to those for the overall slice of the HR Database, they are different in one important respect. Database statistical functions are used for the departmental calculations, whereas regular Lotus 1-2-3 statistical functions are used for the overall calculations. Database statistical functions allow you to search the database for only those records that match some predetermined criterion. For each of the departments, the criterion is already typed onto the worksheet (e.g., the criterion for the Data Processing Department is in cells A21..A22).

Begin the required calculations for the Data Processing Department by calculating the hours lost due to absenteeism in B23. Use the database statistical function @DSUM for this calculation. The general form of this database statistical function is:

@DSUM(input,offset,criterion)

The first argument--input--refers to the worksheet area of the database. In this case, the area of the database is A103..G224, including the field names at the top of each column of data.

The second argument--offset--specifies how many columns removed from the left-most column of the input range Lotus 1-2-3 is to operate on. Go to the database on your worksheet and count from the second column to the column for Yearly Absences (the number of hours lost). The first column is considered zero (0) as you count; thus, begin by counting the second column as one (1).

The third argument--criterion--refers to the area of the worksheet in which the selected field names with their accompanying codes are located. For the departmental analyses, use the first two entries--the label DEPARTMENT and the name of the department--in column A for each department. For the Data Processing Department, the criterion is located at

A21..A22. Proceed by entering the database statistical function @DSUM in its appropriate form in B23. (If you need more information about the database statistical functions, you may wish to review the Analysis section in Chapter 4.)

The number of days lost (B24) is calculated for the Data Processing Department just as it was for the overall group of employees. To calculate the Number (N) of employees for B25, use another database statistical function, @DCOUNT. It is formulated very similarly to the database statistical function @DSUM; however, you may use a zero (0) offset in the database statistical function @DCOUNT for counting the number of employees in the Data Processing Department, since the particular column you count is not important. You are merely counting the number of records that match the criterion of the Data Processing Department.

Again you will use a four-month period for the number of workdays; therefore, type 88 into cell B26. The rate for the department is calculated similarly to the rate for the overall group. Its formula should be entered in B27.

The cost of wages (B28) requires another database statistical function--@DSUM. The input area remains the same, and the criterion remains the same. The offset changes since you want Lotus 1-2-3 to sum data from the column called Absenteeism Cost. Review the database and count from the second column of the database the number of the column occupied by Absenteeism Cost.

The next three calculations (Cost of Wages, Cost of Benefits, and Total Cost) required for the Data Processing Department correspond to those of the overall group of employees.

To calculate the % of Total Employees in a specific department, enter in cell A31 a formula that divides the number of employees in this department by the total number of employees.

To calculate the % Absenteeism Cost (A32), divide Total Cost (for this department) by the Total Cost (for all absenteeism for this slice of the database):

+B30/B19

After having completed the calculations for the Data Processing Department, continue with the calculations for the remaining departments. Note that you may either <u>enter these formulas directly with Lotus 1-2-3 in the Ready mode</u> or <u>copy the formulas from the Data Processing Department to the remaining departments</u>.

If you opt to take the latter action (i.e., copying the formulas), you will have to modify the formulas slightly for the Data Processing Department in order to correctly copy the formulas. The required modification is to indicate to Lotus 1-2-3 that certain values are absolute.

Recall that you may indicate that a cell address is absolute by typing dollar signs ($) in front of the column and row addresses (e.g., $A$103). You will need to do this for only selected parts of the formulas for the Data Processing Department. Thus, considerable care must be taken in editing the formulas if you do copy them.

For example, you will want to make the address of the input argument of the database statistical functions absolute. This area of the worksheet remains constant or absolute. However, the address of the criterion varies from one department to another. You will want to allow Lotus 1-2-3 to change this address as you copy the formula. Thus, an absolute designation for the criterion address is inappropriate. Only parts of the formulas for calculating the percentage of absenteeism cost and the percentage of total employees in a given department require absolute addresses as well.

Whichever course of action you take, continue to complete the output screen for each of the identified departments.

Saving Your Worksheets

Save your work onto the Working Diskette by using the appropriate Lotus 1-2-3 File commands. (For assistance in using the File commands, consult Chapter 2.)

Printing the Results

Before beginning to print the results, check to see that you have edited cell A3 and typed your name after the word **Name:**. Print the output screen by establishing a range of cells A1..C97. Include the C column in your printed results to assure that Lotus 1-2-3 prints the entire title in cell A2. (You may seek assistance in printing the results by consulting the section on Lotus 1-2-3 Print Commands in Chapter 2.)

Analyzing the Results

You may now evaluate the overall absenteeism rates and costs of the hospital as well as the variances among the selected departments. In the space provided, answer the questions at the end of this chapter. Then tear out that page, attach it to the printed results, and turn both in to your instructor.

Endnotes

1. <u>1986-1987 Source Book of Health Insurance Data</u> (Washington, DC: Health Insurance Association of America, 1987), p. 61.

2. See, for example, Arthur W. Sherman, Jr., George Bohlander, and Herbert J. Chruden, <u>Managing Human Resources</u>, Eighth Edition (Cincinnati, OH: South-Western Publishing Company, 1988), pp. 621-623.

3. For an explanation of the formula, see Arthur W. Sherman, Jr., George Bohlander, and Herbert J. Chruden, <u>Managing Human Resources</u>, Eighth Edition (Cincinnati, OH: South-Western Publishing Company, 1988), pp. 621-623.

Questions

1. Evaluate the overall absenteeism rate.

2. Which departments have a relatively better absenteeism rate? What evidence suggests this?

3. Which departments have a poorer absenteeism rate? What evidence suggests this?

4. What recommendations can you make to the HR Department as a result of this audit?

CHAPTER 18
INTERNATIONAL HUMAN RESOURCES MANAGEMENT

Lotus 1-2-3 applications in this chapter:

Command Menus
   FILE
   PRINT
   COPY
   DATA QUERY

Chapter Outline

Background of the Exercise
Retrieving SKILLS
Output
Screen
Input Screen
Analysis
Saving Your Worksheets
Printing the Results
Analyzing the Results

The international business market is still undergoing considerable change. Recent developments have included the expansion of foreign businesses into real estate and manufacturing within the United States. Whereas, in the past, many United States companies used international manufacturing plants to reduce the costs of manufacturing goods for the United States market, these businesses are now developing foreign markets for the sale of United States goods and services. As the world business market continues to expand, there is little doubt that there will be additional changes.

Among the factors that have led to changes in international business practices has been the relative cost of goods and services in the United States market compared with their cost in a foreign market. These costs have led foreign manufacturers to initiate manufacturing operations within the United States. Another factor is the higher level of development of some foreign markets. Recent economic growth around the world has meant that previously less developed countries have gained greater purchasing power. Some United States businesses have begun to respond to this increased purchasing power by expanding the market for their goods and services in these developing countries.

Background of the Exercise

The parent company of Metro Hospital is considering the health-care business opportunity which is beginning to emerge in parts of the world that have increasingly larger disposable incomes. Therefore, it has asked that each of its subsidiaries assess the available skills of their professional and managerial staffs. The parent company is particularly interested in the employees' language skills and attitudes that make an employee favorable to an international assignment. Since Latin America is a possible location for the parent company's operations, Spanish is a language skill in which it is particularly interested.

As a part of its skills analysis, Metro Hospital has data on languages other than English which its employees speak and write. It also has information about travel abroad and previous work abroad. The HR staff believes that travel abroad is some indication of an attitude which may lead to an employee's accepting an international job assignment.

Using its HR Database, the staff intends to extract the names and related information of (1) exempt employees who have traveled abroad and who speak Spanish, (2) exempt employees who have worked abroad, and (3) exempt employees who have worked abroad and speak Spanish.

Retrieving SKILLS

Retrieve the Lotus 1-2-3 file called SKILLS from your HR Data Diskette. Then replace the HR Data Diskette with your Working Diskette.

Output Screen

The output screen for this chapter covers cells A1..I42, and consists of the field names that may be used as database criteria (see Exhibit 18-1). These criteria are located at A7..I8. Also included in the output screen are three sections that correspond to each of the three areas in which the staff intends to extract information about Metro's employees.

The first output section is the area A13..I19, which corresponds to the staff's interest in exempt employees who have traveled abroad and speak Spanish. The second output section is the area A22..I33, which corresponds to the staff's interest in exempt employees who have worked abroad. The third output section is the area A35..I42, which corresponds to the staff's third interest: exempt employees who have worked abroad and speak Spanish.

Input Screen

The input screen is located at cells A44..I167 and includes the following fields from the database: Name, Race, Sex, Job Title, Exempt [status], Language Spoken, Language Written, International Travel, and International Work. The codes for Exempt, International Travel, and International Work are "Y" for Yes and "N" for No. The codes for languages are written as the specific language, e.g., Spanish.

Exhibit 18-1

SKILLS
International Human Resources Management
NAME:

OUTPUT

Criterion
         NAME   RACE SEX JOB TITLE EXEMPT SPOKEN WRITTEN TRAVEL WORK

Output - Exempt + Spanish + International Travel
         NAME   RACE SEX JOB TITLE EXEMPT SPOKEN WRITTEN TRAVEL WORK

Output - Exempt + International Work
         NAME   RACE SEX JOB TITLE EXEMPT SPOKEN WRITTEN TRAVEL WORK

Output - Exempt + International Work + Spanish
         NAME   RACE SEX JOB TITLE EXEMPT SPOKEN WRITTEN TRAVEL WORK

Analysis

   Your task is to analyze the potential for providing the parent company with employees who are willing to accept an assignment at a Latin
American subsidiary. You will make three searches of the database in order
to obtain information about (1) exempt employees who have traveled abroad
and who speak Spanish, (2) exempt employees who have worked abroad, and
(3) exempt employees who have worked abroad and speak Spanish.

   To extract records of exempt employees who have traveled abroad and
who speak Spanish, begin by entering the appropriate codes below the
criteria labels in cells A8..I8. Review the codes as described in the Input Screen section of this chapter. You may also wish to review the codes
as they are recorded beneath the field names in the slice of the HR Database contained in the SKILLS data file.

   To make the criteria with their codes easier to read, enter the
codes with the Lotus 1-2-3 symbol ^, which results in their being centered
within the cell. (For assistance, review the section on Values and Labels
in Chapter 2.)

   Then "create a database." Use the area A8..I9 as the criterion
range. The input range should include the single row of field names just
above the first employee record of this slice of the database, and the
output range should be A14..I19. Then extract the records of exempt employees who speak Spanish and who have traveled abroad.

   To change the codes of the criteria for the next database query,
quit the Lotus 1-2-3 database command menu. Notice that the next section
of the output screen at A22..I33 calls for all exempt employees with international work experience. Go to row 9 and use the Lotus 1-2-3 Range
command menu to erase the codes that you will not need for this particular
database query. The field name labels are protected and should be left
just as they are in row 8.

   Now enter the necessary codes to extract records of exempt employees
who have worked abroad. When you return to the Lotus 1-2-3 database command menu, you need only change the output range prior to extracting the
records that correspond to the criterion as you just modified it. After
typing /DQO (DATA QUERY OUTPUT), press the Escape key to erase the previously stored output range. Then type the new output range, A23..I33. You
are now ready to extract the records of exempt employees who have worked
abroad.

   The final database query is for records of exempt employees who have
worked abroad and who speak Spanish. After quitting the database command
menu, change the criteria codes. Be sure to change the stored output range
prior to extracting the last set of records. The final output range that
you should use is A36..I42. Once you have extracted this set of employee
records, you may print the results.

Saving Your Worksheets

Save your work onto the Working Diskette by using the appropriate Lotus 1-2-3 File commands. (For assistance in using the File commands, consult Chapter 2.)

Printing the Results

Before beginning to print the results, check to see that you have edited cell A3 and typed your name after the word **Name:**. Print the output screen by establishing a range of cells A1..I39. (You may seek assistance in printing the results by consulting the section on Lotus 1-2-3 Print Commands in Chapter 2.)

Analyzing the Results

You may now evaluate Metro Hospital's potential for providing its parent company with employees who are willing to accept an assignment at a Latin American subsidiary. In the space provided, answer the questions at the end of this chapter. Then tear out that page, attach it to the printed results, and turn both in to your instructor.

Questions

1. Which employees are most likely to accept an international work assignment?

2. What additional steps should you take prior to sending this information to the headquarters office?

3. In what other ways may a skills-related database be helpful?